THE WORLD OF DON QUIXOTE

THE WORLD OF

$\mathcal{D}$ON $\mathcal{Q}$UIXOTE

RICHARD L. PREDMORE

HARVARD UNIVERSITY PRESS

CAMBRIDGE, MASSACHUSETTS

For Pat, who has shared all my Spanish adventures

I began to write *The World of Don Quixote* in English in 1956. I had not progressed very far when it became clear to me that none of the extant English translations of Cervantes' masterpiece could be the source of the many passages I needed to quote. Over and over again I found key words and phrases of the Spanish text absent from the English translations. Many of the omissions and inconsistencies of these translations might be explained on stylistic grounds, but plainly they would not serve my purpose. Faced with this problem, I decided to write the study in Spanish, thus making it possible to present reliable quotations without the awkwardness of constant shuttling between English text and Spanish quotation. I finished the study on sabbatical leave in Spain, and published it in Madrid in 1958.

Since then many friends and colleagues have urged me to bring out an English version, alleging that it would be of interest to some fraction of the general reading public and particularly useful to those professors and students who study in English translation selected masterpieces of European literature. I have finally reconciled myself to this project, despite the vexing problem of handling the numerous quotations required. I have been helped to this decision by considering that the original Spanish edition is available to any readers disposed to question the accuracy of the Cervantine texts reproduced in the study.

All the translated passages from *Don Quixote* cited in this edition are mine. They are not all equally felicitous, but I use them consistently, and I believe that in most cases they support my argument almost as effectively as the original Spanish. Since I have not translated and published the entire *Don Quixote*, I cannot give page references for the passages quoted. I locate them for the reader only by part and chapter (thus: I. 3). If this kind of identification does not facilitate quick reference to the context of the quoted passages, it is at least useful in showing approximately how they are distributed through the novel.

In preparing this new version of *The World of Don Quixote*, I have considered the viewpoints expressed by the reviewers of the first edition, and have added or altered something here and there. In the main, however, it stands today on virtually the same grounds as it did in 1958. Since that date I have read a number of valuable books and articles on *Don Quixote*, but they have not changed substantially the views I hold on the six themes I chose to treat in my study.

It is my pleasure to express here my appreciation to the Duke University Council on Research for helping me in the preparation of this edition, as they did in the first.

Richard L. Predmore

Durham, North Carolina
January 1966

The object of the present study is to explore in a brief, clear book the large and complex world created by Cervantes in *Don Quixote*. I say "created," perhaps unnecessarily, so that no one will begin the reading of this book under the misapprehension that I attempt to deal with the historical world of sixteenth-century Spain. I take the quixotic world just as seriously as one could take the historical world, but I do not compare them. And I do not mean to suggest by this that it would be improper or profitless to compare them, but only that to do so has not been my purpose.

In principle, I have tried to take into account everything that Cervantes put into his novelistic world. By this I mean that I have not taken the liberty, as some critics have, of deciding that certain incidents or interpolated stories should be ignored as matter extraneous to the proper composition of *Don Quixote*. In practice, of course, one cannot in a book of these dimensions take complete inventory of a world as spacious as that of Cervantes' masterpiece. From among the numerous elements that compose it, I have chosen those that seem to me absolutely essential, and those I have studied as scrupulously as I know how. Perhaps this approach may be likened to a series of test borings calculated to reveal treasures hidden from surface observation.

In *Don Quixote*, as in many literary works, certain motifs betray their omnipresence by a kind of linguistic radiation. For example, the language of passions like love and jealousy extends beyond the concrete cases of such passions treated by the author; the extremely varied language marshaled to express the doubts and confusions of man confronting the complexities of reality is more copious than the specific cases of error or imperfect interpretation. So it is that I have devoted many pages to the study of words and phrases which seem to me to contribute notably to the total impression created by Cervantes' novel. In a work as extensive as *Don Quixote*, a handful of examples does not suffice to establish the essential nature of this or that motif. Guided by this conviction, I may have erred on the side of too many examples. In any case, the examples displayed are almost always fewer than the ones collected.

This book is not a survey of what has been written about *Don Quixote,* nor is it an interpretation put together like a patchwork quilt out of fragments of other interpretations. It rests on many close readings of the Cervantine text and many hours of study and reflection. In this sense it is original. But, of course, many parts of my interpretation, taken separately, may be found in the writings of other scholars. If I quote them but sparingly, it is in part because I have wanted to reduce to a minimum the distraction of footnotes, and in part because I have wanted to make Cervantes the supreme authority for what I have to say. I have attempted to heed all the data he provides. To study enchantment, for example, I have taken into account every case of enchantment and every statement about enchantment recorded in Cervantes' novel, and not merely those that seemed to fit some possibly premature hypothesis. In a word, my aspiration has been to demonstrate as thoroughly as possible the soundness of my description of Don Quixote's world. One of the features of that world, which I hope I have demonstrated, is its harmony and inner consistency.

The perspicacious reader may note that one or two chapters of this book might well have been written in the language of modern psychology. But that specialized language is unnatural to me, and besides, some of its intentions might prove rebellious to mine. I have tried, therefore, to content myself with the unspecialized language of general culture.

CONTENTS

1 · Literature and Life   1

2 · Adventures   17

3 · Enchantment   36

4 · Reality   53

5 · Illusions   84

6 · Madness and Recovered Sanity   98

   Epilogue   128

   Index   131

THE WORLD OF DON QUIXOTE

1 · LITERATURE AND LIFE

EADERS OF *Don Quixote* can hardly fail to be
impressed by the enormous amount of literature
which in its pages is read, written, lived, discussed,
alluded to, and represented. In the past, critics and scholars
were inclined to examine this literary material, if they examined it at all, as though it were merely literary baggage
which, when checked, would reveal where Cervantes had
been and what he had acquired in the world of literature.
Sometimes this kind of examination has been rewarding,
but obviously it leaves untouched a very important question: Does the literary matter contained in *Don Quixote*
fulfill any essential function, or is it simply illustration,
adornment, evidence of Cervantes' sources?

Today most critics would insist that literature does fulfill
an essential function in *Don Quixote*, but they would not
all agree on just what that function is. Small wonder. The
book is large and complex, and the functions are many. The
purpose of this chapter is to identify and interpret the essential ones. The most evident is to motivate men's lives and
to provide them with the illusions by which, in part, they
live. This is all too obviously true of Don Quixote's life, but
it is so important that we shall have to return to it more
than once in the course of this book. It was the literature of
chivalry that transformed the Manchegan knight's life so
radically. But his life is not the only one affected by literature, nor is the literature of knight-errantry the only kind
to affect men's lives. Cervantes' masterpiece suggests that
any kind of reading is potentially revolutionary. In chapter
6 of Part I, for example, Don Quixote's niece urges the
Priest to burn her uncle's pastoral novels as well as his

books of chivalry, lest he take it into his head to imitate the pastoral life. Her fears proved to be well founded, and no fewer than three other groups of people left their prosaic lives for a sojourn in Arcadia. Grisóstomo belonged to one of these groups, and it is not without significance that books were carried on his funeral litter. Consider also the case of Ginés de Pasamonte. When he boasted that the publication of his life would usher in a bad year for *Lazarillo de Tormes* (I. 22), he revealed that even the picaresque novel might help to create a pattern for men's lives.

When Don Quixote sallied forth upon the roads of Spain to live a life reborn in the realm of books, two worlds were set in contrast: the given world of Cervantes' day and the created world of books. Each of these was apt to suggest a different interpretation of reality: castle or inn, high-born maiden or lowly prostitute, enchanted helmet or barber's basin, noble righting of wrong or unfortunate meddling. And each interpretation had at least the validity of enabling a man somehow to live by it. The establishment of this contrast between literature and life provides the principal basis for the once widely held opinion that Cervantes was seeking to discover the true nature of reality. Undoubtedly, it also underlies Américo Castro's claim that in *Don Quixote* reality is always an aspect of man's experience.[1] Whether these interpretations are correct or not, it seems clear that Cervantes was able to explore the relationship of reality to human experience by setting literature in contrast to life. This, then, is another and not improbable way of describing the function of literature in *Don Quixote*.

There are other more or less acceptable partial interpretations of that function. Most, if not all of them, involve the establishment of some kind of relationship between literature and life. Since everything in *Don Quixote* is really lit-

1. *Miguel de Cervantes Saavedra, Homenaje de Ínsula en el cuarto centenario de su nacimiento, 1547-1947* (Madrid, 1947), p. 35.

erature, this relationship is an artistic illusion achieved by establishing two fictional levels so separated that the difference which separates them seems to the reader to be the difference between literature and life. This is a fundamental aspect of the structure of the book, and the one whose study appears to offer the largest rewards. As we proceed, it will become increasingly clear that literature is perhaps the most important feature of the environment in which Don Quixote and Sancho are made to live, and that living in this special environment contributes greatly to the air of autonomous reality they so convincingly wear.[2]

On the first page of the Prologue to Part I, Cervantes tells his readers that he is not the father but the stepfather of Don Quixote. This is the first clue that the knight's relation to Cervantes is not to be the straightforward one of literary creature to literary creator. A page or two farther on, after explaining to a friend the difficulty he experiences in writing his prologue, he states that he has about decided to leave his hero buried in the archives of La Mancha. The friend, in urging Cervantes on with his task, speaks of "your famous Don Quixote." Finally, Cervantes speaks of the "history of the famous Don Quixote de la Mancha, who, in the opinion of all the inhabitants of the district of Montiel, was the chastest lover and the bravest knight to be seen in those parts in many a year." A few lines beyond the ones just quoted, Cervantes bespeaks the reader's gratitude for acquaintance with "the famous Sancho Panza." From all this we may deduce that Cervantes was not the original author of *Don Quixote* and that his heroes were already well known in La Mancha.

In the first chapter of Part I, Cervantes says of Don Quixote's real name: "They will tell you that his surname

2. See Joseph E. Gillet, "The Autonomous Character in Spanish and European Literature," *Hispanic Review*, 24 (1956), 179-190. Pp. 179-180 refer to the autonomous character in *Don Quixote*.

is Quijada or Quesada, although in this there is some difference of opinion among the authors who write of the
matter." Then for a number of chapters Cervantes buttress-
es this or that statement with phrases like "as is believed,"
"as is understood," "there are authors who say," "it is
believed." In addition to these impersonal sources there is
an unidentified "I": "but what I have been able to ascertain
of this matter, and what I have found written in the annals
of La Mancha. . . ." Finally, in chapter 9, the unspecified
sources are reduced to one: Cide Hamete Benengeli,[3] an
Arabic historian and the true author of the life of Don
Quixote.[4] Cervantes, having found and bought the Arabic
manuscript in Toledo, is the one who caused it to be translated and published. In his own words he is merely Don
Quixote's stepfather.

As soon as the existence of Benengeli is established, Cervantes suggests that if there are any reservations about the
truth of Don Quixote's history,[5] it is the fault of this infidel.
On one occasion he declares a whole chapter apocryphal,
although without specifically blaming Benengeli (II. 5).
On at least three other occasions he twits him about some
minor defect in his narration.[6] For the most part, however,
he praises him, as do also a number of characters in the
novel.[7] But whether censured or praised, the important consideration is how faithful he was to the lives he reported.

3. Actually there occur after chapter 9 a few more mentions of un-
specified sources like the ones already quoted. Predominantly, however,
Cide Hamete Benengeli is the authority for everything about Don
Quixote and Sancho.

4. This device is copied from the romances of chivalry, where it
seems to have been used to increase their credibility. As we shall see,
Cervantes carries it far beyond anything found in chivalric literature.

5. The Spanish word is *historia*, which may mean either "story" or
"history." Professor Bruce W. Wardropper argues convincingly for the
second meaning of *historia* as applied by Cervantes to his novel. See his
"*Don Quixote*: Story or History," *Modern Philology*, 63 (1965), 1-11.

6. The suggestion that Benengeli might not always respect the truth
is found in I. 9. The other ironical criticisms are found in II. 10, 60, 68.

7. See II. 3, 40, 59, 61, 74.

That is to say, Cervantes insists that we consider the difference between the lives of his characters and the written account of them.

According to Cervantes' fiction, everything we know about the characters who people his novel we learn from Benengeli. Benengeli tells much of the story unobtrusively, but there are times when he steps out from behind the scenes and plays the role of intruding narrator. Let us glance at the kind of things he says on these occasions, most of which occur in Part II. He may complain about the self-imposed restriction of writing only on Don Quixote and Sancho (II. 44). A run in Don Quixote's stocking may inspire him to cry out against poverty (II. 44). He may confirm his characters' interpretation of the name "Countess Trifaldi" (II. 38). Most often he is concerned with his characters themselves: He thinks Don Quixote might have laughed on seeing Sancho tossed in a blanket if he hadn't been so angry (I. 17). He debates the authenticity of Don Quixote's report of his descent into the cave of Montesinos (II. 24). Reflecting on the conduct of the Duke and Duchess, he concludes that the mockers are as mad as the mocked (II. 70). He confirms the notion that Sancho was a charitable soul (II. 54). He exclaims that he would have given his best mantle for the chance to have witnessed the scene in which Don Quixote leads the distressed Doña Rodríguez into his bedroom (II. 48). He is tremendously proud that his writing proved equal to the task of reporting Don Quixote's deeds (II. 74). The effect of all this obvious concern for his characters and for the efficacy of his attempt to present them faithfully is to enhance the reader's impression that the characters lived lives independent of their literary embodiment, which must inevitably fall short of perfect truth.

Before we finish with Benengeli, let us consider the oft-repeated phrase "the history says." This phrase and its variants occur some nineteen times in the novel.[8] Since the "history" was written by Benengeli, the phrase is only another way of appealing to his authority. In an original and convincing study of *Don Quixote*[9] Professor R. S. Willis, Jr., makes some interesting comments on Cervantes' use of "the history says." Willis' essay studies the openings and closings of the chapters in *Don Quixote*. Among other things it shows clearly that the chapter divisions are an authentic part of the original composition, that conventional chapters are incompatible with Cervantes' vision of life as a constant flow, and that by a variety of stylistic devices Cervantes was able, in effect, to annul most chapter divisions and maintain the narrative flow of his text. Willis finds, however, that there exist a number of chapter junctions that are logically absurd. At or very near the point of these textual breaks one always finds the phrase "the history says." Three quotations will show how Willis interprets these facts:

In contradistinction to the material manifestations of the *Historia,* the real, the true *Historia*, that floats inaccessible in the Empyrean, cannot but be perfect and whole, as is all incorporeal spirit. . . . And it is to this perfect whole that appeal is made by variants of the phrase, *Dice la historia,* at each of the points, which in turn are the only real points, where the Cervantine text is interrupted in its flow. To change the figure, the web of text is cut, and with considerable display, too; but simultaneously the very words that did the cutting turn into threads that conjoin both termini of the severed fabric with the web of the transcendent Text, that is mythical, perfect, and whole. Or, in psychological terms, the reader is reminded at each interruption, by the interrupting words, that

8. The Spanish phrase is "dice la historia." See I. 9, 20, 26; II. 2, 14, 17, 33, 40, 44, 47, 50, 52, 53, 56, 61, 64.
9. *The Phantom Chapters of the Quijote* (New York, 1953).

there exists a History of Don Quixote which formal devices cannot divide into segments. . . . Furthermore, it is not by accident that at the very same points of textual fragmentation, the substance of the novel spans the fissures from beneath, since, as was pointed out, there is no break whatsoever in the doing or the being of the novelistic personages at the illogical points where Cervantes elected to effect a division of the text into formal units.[10]

While examination shows Professor Willis' statement of the facts to be altogether accurate, it seems to me that the same cannot be said for his interpretation of them. Unless we assume that the translator did violence to Benengeli's text, there is no "transcendent text" but only the one we know. The real contrast established by Cervantes is between this text and life. In Willis' reference to the transcendent text as "incorporeal spirit" we might see a vague and metaphorical allusion to life, if it were not for his frequent return to the distinction between a perfect and imperfect text. When we remember that "the history says" is only another way of saying "Cide Hamete says," [11] and that Cervantes and Cide Hamete himself show concern for the accuracy of the latter's *History*, it becomes evident that the contrast on which Cervantes insists is that between life and any attempt to record it faithfully.

The most obvious means used by Cervantes to keep before his readers the contrast between literature and life is to arrange that his hero go mad from the reading of books. Don Quixote accepts the romances of chivalry as true accounts of real lives. For this he is severely criticized on various occasions. The Canon's remarks may be taken as typical:

10. *Ibid.*, pp. 98, 100.
11. II. 50. Benengeli is mentioned by name on at least 34 different pages of the novel. In the following chapters his name occurs as a substitute for "history" in phrases like "the history says": I. 15, 22; II. 1, 27, 52, 53, 73.

7

Is it possible, my good sir, that the bitter and idle reading of the books of chivalry has had such an effect on you that it has upset your judgment and made you believe that you are enchanted and other things of this kind, as far from being so as falsehood itself from truth? And how is it possible that there be any human understanding capable of believing in the existence of those numberless Amadises, of that multitude of famous knights, of so many emperors of Trebizond, so many Felixmartes of Hyrcania, so many palfreys, so many wandering damsels, so many serpents, so many dragons [I. 49].[12]

If Don Quixote is often criticized for not distinguishing between literature and life, the books that disturbed his wits are just as often censured for lack of verisimilitude—that is, for appearing untrue to life. The best-remembered example of such censure is found in the famous scrutiny of Don Quixote's library (I. 6). Most of the knight's romances of chivalry are condemned to perish by fire for being absurd. Of the three that with certainty escape the fire, the one discussed in most detail is *Tirante el Blanco*. Here is a portion of what the Priest has to say of it: "My friend, I say truly that for its style this is the best book in the world: here knights eat and sleep and die in their beds, and make their wills before they die, and still more things which are lacking in the other books of the kind" (I. 6). From these words it is clear that *Tirante el Blanco* is appreciated for its realism, and that the other romances of chivalry are noted as lacking this realism. It is hardly necessary to remark that Don Quixote eats, sleeps, dies in bed, and makes his will before he dies in the fashion approved by the Priest.

Another occasion when books of chivalry are discussed is after dinner one day at Juan Palomeque's inn (I. 32). Here the Priest tries in vain to persuade the innkeeper that

12. The Priest, the Gentleman in Green, and the Duke's chaplain make similar criticisms: I. 32; II. 1, 16, 31.

such books are full of lies and foolishness. The last notable example of such discussion is found in chapters 47 and 48 of Part I, where the Priest and the Canon from Toledo consider the merits and defects of chivalric literature. Here is a pertinent fragment of a long statement by the Canon: "What beauty can there be, or what proportion of parts to whole or whole to parts, in a book or story in which a sixteen-year-old lad deals a sword-thrust to a giant as tall as a tower and cuts him in two as though he were made of sugar paste; and in which, when they want to describe a battle, after telling us there are a million foes among the enemy, so long as the hero of the book is against them, we must believe willy-nilly that he achieved the victory by the valor of his strong arm alone?" (I. 47). There is a good deal more in the same vein. Most books of chivalry are full of lies, and the lies are not contrived with sufficient art to give them even the outward look of truth.

The romances of chivalry are not the only ones criticized for lack of verisimilitude. In one of the chapters mentioned above, the Priest and the Canon discuss also the Spanish theater of their day and find it lacking in verisimilitude (I. 48). In chapter 33 of Part I the Priest begins to read aloud the story of the *Man Too Curious for His Own Good*. At the end of chapter 35 he pronounces judgment upon it.[13] He likes the way it is told, but considers it neither

13. Willis, in *Phantom Chapters*, p. 43, remarks that this device is not original with Cervantes, having been used at the end of the story of Abindarráez in *La Diana*. In the context of his argument this is correct; in mine it needs amplification. The story of Abindarráez is told as true, not read as literature, and Felicia's favorable judgment of it has to do only with the elegance of the telling. While we are on the subject of interpolated stories, it may be instructive to recall how Mateo Alemán handles the three well-known stories in *Guzmán de Alfarache* (all references are to the edition in Clásicos Castellanos). The story of Ozmín and Daraja is told as true and not discussed at all (I. 175-245); the same thing may be said of the story of Dorido and Clorinia (III. 19-40); like the *Man Too Curious for His Own Good*, the story of Dorotea and Bonifacio is read, but, unlike Cervantes' story, it is not discussed or judged (IV. 142-169). In other words the interpolated stories in *Guzmán de Alfarache* and *La Diana* contribute nothing to the illusion we are studying.

true nor plausible. Earlier in Part I we may read that pastoral literature is likewise unfaithful to truth (I. 27). Throughout Cervantes' novel there is much discussion of literature, and many things are said of it which I shall have no occasion to recall. What is important to my thesis is that literary judgments are often pronounced, and these judgments are almost always concerned, among other things, with verisimilitude. This has the effect of keeping ever before the reader the distinction between literature and life.

Some of the literary discussions of the kind treated above may be viewed with profit as physical scenes. As Priest, Barber, Housekeeper, and Niece busy themselves with the books in Don Quixote's library, handling them, dropping them, tossing them out the window, their very physical presence among the books leads the reader almost insensibly to distinguish between the friends of Don Quixote and those other people who live only in books that may be so handled.[14] The story of the *Man Too Curious for His Own Good* contributes to the same illusion and in the same way. Unlike the personally-related history of the Captive Captain and others of that nature, this is written literature, a manuscript. It is clearly so presented and discussed. It establishes another fictional level, which we regard from the same point of view as the Priest and his listeners. One might say that for a time we sit down beside them and lend them some of our reality. Still another scene contributing to the same effect is the one in which Don Quixote inspects the workings of a printing house in Barcelona (II. 62).

14. The fact that among Don Quixote's books were some published less than a score of years before Cervantes' own novel may have rendered his characters more real to his contemporaries. Cervantes himself has something to say on this subject: "On the other hand, it seemed to me that since among his books there had been found some so modern as *Desengaño de celos* and *Ninfas y pastores de Henares,* his history too must be modern, and even though it were not written down, it was probably present in the memory of the people in his village and in the surrounding region" (I. 9).

Different from the devices already presented but equally calculated to keep the reader from forgetting the distinction between literature and life is the device which lets the characters anticipate or desire that their lives be some day recorded. For Don Quixote an honorable place in literature would represent the recognition and perpetuation of fame. At the time of his first sally he confidently predicts that his as-yet-unperformed deeds will win literary commemoration: "Who doubts but that in ages to come, when the true history of my famous deeds is published, the sage who writes them down will say as follows when he comes to relate my first sally so early in the morning . . ." (I. 2). Shortly after the taking of Mambrino's helmet, Sancho recommends to his master that they undertake to serve some emperor. On this occasion he, too, predicts that their exploits will be recorded for posterity (I. 21). Toward the end of Part I the Priest ironically makes the same prediction (I. 47). Then, in the second chapter of Part II, Sancho reveals to Don Quixote that he has learned from Sansón Carrasco that their adventures have been published in a book. Carrasco himself soon calls on Don Quixote to confirm the exciting news. From this point on, the knight's life is much affected by the realization that he is the subject of a book and also by having to deal with people who have read it. Of this we shall have more to say later. For now let us remark only that the insistent predictions that the lives of knight and squire would some day be written enhance the illusion that their reality is not merely bookish. And in Part II this illusion is developed with some new twists.

Sansón Carrasco was a student full of mischief and mockery. A good part of his conversation was touched with irony, but here are a few of his words that sound quite sincere: "The Bachelor was astonished to hear the manner and mode of Sancho Panza's speech, for though he had read the first history of his master, he never believed Sancho so comical as there described; but now hearing him say will and codicil that cannot be *revolted* instead of will and codicil that cannot be *revoked*, he believed all that he had read of him and confirmed him for one of the most solemn fools of our century, and said to himself that such a pair of madmen as master and man could not have been seen in the world before" (II. 7). Direct observation of master and squire confirms the essential truth of their written history. This device is anticipated in the middle of Part I, where Cardenio responds to the Priest's judgment of Don Quixote's strange behavior with these words: "It certainly is . . . and so rare and never-seen that I don't know whether a person wishing to invent such behavior in a story could muster the talent to succeed" (I. 30). Cardenio clearly implies that only by seeing Don Quixote with his own eyes could he believe in his existence. In Part II the author informs us that the outlaw Roque Guinart was pleased to encounter Don Quixote, so that he could check by personal observation the truth of the stories he had heard (II. 60). In all cases the knight's presence and conduct confirm the essential truth of his published life.

Nowhere in the novel is the illusion of Don Quixote's and Sancho's autonomous reality more successfully sustained than in the opening chapters of Part II. Here most convincingly knight and squire seem to stand outside the book that gave them life. At the beginning of chapter 3 Don Quixote is burning with impatience as he waits for Sancho to return with the Bachelor Carrasco, who has read his published history. While awaiting the Bachelor, he tries anxiously to imagine how his history came to be written and whether it was done according to the dictates of truth and propriety. When the Bachelor does arrive, Don Quixote questions him eagerly about his good name, about which of his adventures are narrated, and about much else, including the possibility of a second part to his history. Much later Sancho remarks to the Duchess that his enchantment of Dulcinea is not yet in the history (II. 33). This comment of Sancho's, and Don Quixote's question about a second part, balance a device we noted in Part I: while the reader is reading Part I, the characters in Part I predict that their story will some day be written; while the reader peruses Part II, Don Quixote asks whether there will be a Part II and Sancho tells of an incident as yet unrecorded.

In the early chapters of Part II Cervantes makes artistic capital even out of the minor slips of Part I. For example, when Carrasco asks Sancho how he managed to ride his stolen ass before it was recovered, Sancho explains what really happened and then remarks that if it is not so related in the history, it must be the fault of the historian or the printer (II. 4). Another occasion where Sancho refers to possible betrayal at the printer's occurs at the time of his first conversation with the Duchess. When the latter asks Sancho whether his master is not the same knight about whom a history has been printed, Sancho answers, "He's the very one, my lady . . . and that squire of his, who is or ought to be in that history, and who is called Sancho Panza, is myself, unless they changed me in the cradle, I mean, in the press" (II. 30). In a penetrating essay on *Don Quixote* Leo Spitzer quotes a portion of these words and then comments: "In such passages, Cervantes willingly destroys the artistic illusion; he, the puppeteer, lets us see the strings of his puppet-show; see, reader, this is not life, but a stage, a book: art; recognize the life-giving power of the artist as a thing distinct from life." [15] The context of this quotation makes me uncertain whether Spitzer interprets Sancho's words as I do. Much of the context stresses the self-glorification of the Renaissance artist. Cervantes does, indeed, exhibit the strings of his puppet show, but less, I think, to make the reader "recognize the life-giving power of the artist" than to maintain the illusion that his heroes are real

15. *Linguistics and Literary History* (Princeton University Press, 1948), pp. 70-71.

13

no matter how they may have fared at the hands of printers and historians. The self-expressed concern of knight and squire over this matter is part of what makes them seem so real. Let us look briefly at a few more examples.

In chapter 8 of Part II Don Quixote and Sancho discuss the latter's past embassy to Dulcinea. Don Quixote, irritated by Sancho's crude vision of her, attributes it to evil enchanters, and then expresses this concern about his printed history: "and so I am afraid that in that history of my deeds which they say is now in print, if by chance the author is a sage hostile to me, he has probably put one thing for another, mixing one truth with a thousand lies, amusing himself by relating actions other than those required in the sequence of a true history." On this same occasion Sancho speculates that he too has probably fared ill in the history. In chapter 59 of Part II, two gentlemen show Don Quixote and Sancho a copy of the second part of their history in the false version by Avellaneda. Both are misrepresented in it. Sancho well expresses their concern for the truth of their lives when he observes: "Believe me, gentlemen . . . the Sancho and the Don Quixote of that history must be different people from those who figure in the one composed by Cide Hamete Benengeli, who are we two: my master, valiant, discreet, and in love; and myself, simple, comical, and no glutton nor drunkard." As knight and squire return again and again to the question of the faithfulness of their published lives to the lives they know they have lived, the reader is led ever more surely to accept them as men, real and autonomous.[16]

16. Many readers have testified to this impression. No one bears more eloquent witness to it than the late Miguel de Unamuno, who so often exalted both the merit and the reality of Don Quixote over those of his creator. Although it is not at all clear that he meant it so, this is high tribute to Cervantes' art. For some of Unamuno's remarks on the subject, see the Prologue and also p. 279 of his *Vida de Don Quijote y Sancho* (3d ed., Austral; Madrid: Espasa-Calpe, 1938); and p. 233 of his *Del sentimiento trágico de la vida* (Austral; Madrid: Espasa-Calpe, 1937).

As early as the Prologue to Part I Cervantes invites the reader to believe that Don Quixote and Sancho really existed. There and in the opening chapters he alludes to unidentified sources of information about them. In chapter 9 these vague and varied sources are reduced to one principal source: the Arabic historian, Cide Hamete Benengeli. In the same chapter and occasionally thereafter, Cervantes suggests that Benengeli might sometimes betray the trust of a true historian. In this fashion Cervantes tries to induce his readers to accept a difference between the lives of his characters and whatever may be written about them. Benengeli in person, and as represented by the phrase "the history says," helps to reinforce the same distinction. Don Quixote, by accepting the romances of chivalry as true accounts of historical lives, prepares the way for further reinforcement of the illusion. He is criticized for not distinguishing between literature and life. The books that addled his brains are censured for, among other reasons, lacking verisimilitude. Other written works are read, handled, discussed, and judged. Adverse judgments always point to a common failing: the condemned works are not true to life. Perhaps the illusion we are studying is best served by the self-expressed concern of the characters for their published lives. In Part I they anticipate the immortality of bookish fame; in Part II they face the achievement of that fame. The achievement fills them with both pride and anxiety. Needless to say, the anxiety is for the faithfulness of their written lives to the lives they know they have lived.

By now it must be apparent that there are really two fundamental ways of looking at literature in *Don Quixote*. One way makes it an essential feature of the world in which Cervantes causes his characters to live: Don Quixote and a number of other characters are deeply influenced by the books they have read. Both in anticipation and in fulfillment, the protagonists are profoundly affected by the book of their own lives, even by its apocryphal version. Another way of looking at literature makes it a device for the achievement of an artistic illusion: by presenting Don Quixote and Sancho Panza as distinct from whatever has been, is, or may be written about them, Cervantes has invested them with an air of autonomy perhaps unequaled in the history of the novel.

*N*OW THAT WE have seen how, within the world of his enduring novel, Cervantes established two fictional levels so separated that the distance between them appears to the reader to be the difference between literature and life, we shall go on to Don Quixote's adventures. The first and most obvious thing about them is that they are the visible manifestations of the knight's madness, which consists precisely in his inability to recognize the difference between life and literature. But Don Quixote's attempt to carry the fictions of chivalry into the society of his contemporaries reveals more than the workings of his madness. Among other things, it reveals something of the nature and inner workings of the created world in which they occur and of which they are a part.

In Part I Don Quixote's adventures arise directly out of his attempts to imitate one or another of the activities typical of the knights-errant about whom he had read so much. All are the product of a chance encounter and a bookish recollection.[1] All of them involve battle or the probable risk of battle. According to these criteria, the adventures of Part I are: the muleteers (chap. 3), Andrés (chap. 4), the merchants from Toledo (chap. 4), the windmills (chap. 8), the

---

1. Seven of the adventures that I am about to list are accompanied or preceded by specific reminders that Don Quixote's conduct is in large part imitation of bookish models. Here is one: "Scarcely had Don Quixote spied them [the merchants from Toledo], when he imagined them to be material for a new adventure; and it seemed to him they came most opportunely for him to imitate faithfully one of the adventures about which he had read in his books" (I. 4). See also I. 2, 8, 10, 18, 19, 20. These are merely the references that apply to seven specific adventures of Don Quixote in Part I. There are many more that apply to episodes we have not classified as adventures.

battle with the Basque (chaps. 8-9), the two flocks of sheep (chap. 18), the dead body (chap. 19), the fulling mills (chap. 20), Mambrino's helmet (chap. 21), the galley slaves (chap. 22), the wineskins (chap. 35), and the penitents (chap. 52).[2]

One particular kind of knightly activity was imitated in each of these adventures. To begin with, all aspirants to knighthood were obliged to stand vigil over their arms. The battle with the muleteers was provoked by their interference with Don Quixote's vigil. All true knights were committed to succor the weak and oppressed. Don Quixote's desire to fulfill this part of his mission gave rise to the following adventures: Andrés, the Basque, the two flocks of sheep, the dead body, the galley slaves, the wineskins, and the penitents. True knights were supposed to combat evil. The windmills were evil giants. Knights were wont to face and explore mysterious situations that appeared to promise adventures: the fulling mills. One knight sometimes fought another over the question of whose lady was the more beautiful: the merchants from Toledo. Occasionally a knight fought for equipment badly needed: Mambrino's helmet. All of these adventures involved real or attempted battle except those of Andrés and the fulling mills, and even in them Don Quixote invited battle.

Let us examine these adventures to see how closely the world of *Don Quixote* is policed by moral principles. More than forty years ago Américo Castro stated and supported the opinion that one finds a considerable moral order in Cervantes' novels and stories.[3] In recent years Castro has radically modified his earlier views.[4] I summarize them

2. I consider this list complete, but the addition or subtraction of an episode or two (like the bookishly interpreted interview with Maritornes in the starry garret of the inn) would make no difference to my study. In chapters 21 and 50 Don Quixote improvises two brief tales of chivalry, but there he makes no attempt to carry them into the realm of action.

3. See esp. chap. 3 of his *El pensamiento de Cervantes* (Madrid, 1925).

4. See pp. xvi-xxv of his recent Prólogo to *El ingenioso hidalgo Don Quijote de la Mancha* (Mexico, Editorial Porrúa, 1963).

here not because I agree with them, nor much less to dispute ground long since abandoned, but because seeing Don Quixote's adventures in their light contributes to our understanding of the quixotic world. The pertinent part of Castro's earlier discussion may be summarized very briefly as follows: Everywhere in Cervantes' fiction one may discover in operation what Castro calls the "doctrine of error." According to this doctrine, Cervantes' characters are punished quite methodically for their errors. If such errors originate in a false interpretation of physical realities, the results always fall somewhere in the range of the comical. If they stem from a false interpretation of moral realities, the consequences are usually tragic. "Death *post errorem*," for example, is the consequence of moral error in the realm of love. This is a reasonable description of a visible tendency in Cervantes' fiction. Yet while it is probably an adequate beginning to Castro's search for Cervantes the moralist, it is neither detailed nor flexible enough to satisfy our inquiry into the fictional world of *Don Quixote*.

For our purposes it will be advantageous to view Don Quixote's adventures first in the light of their success or failure. To avoid, in the case of a few adventures, the disagreement that might arise as to whether they were successes or failures, we shall classify them according to Don Quixote's reaction to them. In other words, when he is pleased with the outcome of an adventure, we may say it is successful; when he is displeased, we may call it a failure.

Don Quixote is clearly successful in his adventure with the muleteers, since their actions fail to prevent him from satisfying his desire to stand watch over his arms and thus prepare himself for the ceremony of being knighted. His second adventure seems to him an immediate success: he has secured justice for the abused shepherd boy Andrés. In this case, however, the knight's satisfaction is lost in chagrin once he learns (I. 31) that his meddling in Andrés' affairs has only made matters worse for the boy. When Don

Quixote attempts to compel the merchants to admit the superiority of Dulcinea's beauty, it wins him a drubbing. The windmill-giants unhorse the knight, but he does the same for the Basque. The adventure of the two flocks of sheep ends in painful defeat. And while Don Quixote is not defeated in the adventure of the dead body, his desire to avenge the death of the man on the litter is frustrated by his discovery that the man died of a pestilent fever. As for the adventure of the fulling mills, it is entirely psychological. We may admire Don Quixote for his courage on that night of fear, but he is utterly disgusted that circumstances which appeared to promise so much yielded nothing but laughter. The adventure of Mambrino's helmet is successful. So is Don Quixote's attempt to free the galley slaves, but they prove ungrateful and leave him bruised in body and spirit. In the somnambulant adventure of the wineskins, Don Quixote thinks he has killed the giant enemy of the Princess Micomicona, but later he is given cause to doubt it. In the encounter with the penitents he is knocked senseless. We may say, then, that of the twelve adventures in Part I three are clearly successful (muleteers, Basque, Mambrino's helmet); six are clearly failures (merchants, windmills, flocks of sheep, dead body, fulling mills, penitents); and three more are essentially failures even though for a time they may wear some semblance of success (Andrés, galley slaves, wineskins).

Are Don Quixote's failures and successes tightly bound to some moral order? By what laws, if any, are rewards and punishments meted out? And are the rewards and punishments proportionate to the conduct rewarded or punished? Another look at the adventures may help to answer these questions.

Earlier we said that at least seven of the adventures in Part I are motivated by Don Quixote's will to succor the weak and oppressed. If there were a moral order designed to reward good intentions, then all would agree that these deserve success. Only one of the seven is fully successful: the Basque. If an accurate reading of reality were necessary for success, how many of the adventures would deserve to succeed? In ten of the twelve adventures, Don Quixote completely misinterprets what he sees before him. Only in those with Andrés and the galley slaves does he register accurately what is before his eyes. But even at such times his perception is limited to the immediate reality, and his intervention is not adequate to the total situation confronted. On the basis of his interpretation of reality, then, none of his adventures merit success; yet three do succeed.

Both the muleteers of chapter 3 and the shepherds of chapter 18 find that Don Quixote's activities interfere with theirs. Don Quixote triumphs over the first and is badly hurt by the second. Of course, Don Quixote did more damage to the second. Is this a clue to some kind of order? Are punishments always graduated to fit the offense? Well, in the adventure of the dead body Don Quixote causes an innocent stranger to break his leg while he himself emerges from the adventure unhurt. We called this adventure a failure. In the battle with the Basque, Don Quixote wins but is painfully wounded. We called this adventure a success. In the adventure with the galley slaves, Don Quixote takes a beating not from those he has wronged but from those he has liberated. It is true that he asked them to do what criminals obviously could not do (return with their chains to El Toboso), but they could have fled without stoning and beating him. In other words, the beating is not merely a punishment for *his* error. It is also an expression of *their* character. And this is typical of the world of *Don Quixote*. In it there are no purely instrumental characters, no rigid principles, no simple explanations. There is room for the operation of chance.

The merchants from Toledo were unarmed, and surely

Don Quixote was more than a match for them. Why was he defeated? Why simply because Rocinante fell. We are told that this was the good luck of the merchants: "if good luck had not caused Rocinante to stumble and fall in the middle of the road, the bold merchant would have fared ill" (I. 4). Why was Don Quixote able to defeat the Basque? Partly because the Basque had trouble with his mule (I. 8), partly because Don Quixote was favored by good luck: "but good luck, which held him in reserve for greater things, twisted the sword of his adversary in such a way that, although it did catch his left shoulder, it did no other harm than to disarm him on that side, carrying away a good part of his helmet with half his ear" (I. 9). How was Don Quixote able to overcome the armed men who were guarding the galley slaves? Partly because his first lunge happened to strike down the one with a gun (I. 22).[5] Among Don Quixote's adventures in Part I, then, there appear to be some random successes and failures. That all the lives in *Don Quixote* are affected at one time or another by the workings of chance or some analogous power is confirmed by passages that are thickly scattered through the novel.[6]

5. The narrator says: "he knocked him to the ground, badly wounded by a lance thrust; and it turned out well for him [Don Quixote], because this was the man with the gun" (I. 22). Actually two guards had guns, but Cervantes seems to have forgotten this, and it is clear that he intended to give good luck a role in Don Quixote's initial success.

6. In the world of *Don Quixote* the role of chance and its analogues is nevertheless subordinate to that of human will. To study them fully here would consume more time and space than is warranted by their role. However, a rapidly acquired sense of their widespread presence can be gained by noting samples of the language used to express them. Take the word *suerte* (luck). It is often found in combinations like these: "luck willed" (I. 22, 27, 41; II. 46); "luck ordained" (I. 15, 27, 33; II. 58, 63, 65); "good luck willed" (I. 27, 39, 41); "bad luck willed" (I. 17, 41); "to let luck run" (I. 21; II. 7); "luck caused" (I. 23); "my luck does not wish" (I. 24); "my scant luck" (I. 24; II. 55); and in others too numerous to record. *Ventura* (chance) and *fortuna* (fortune) sometimes replace *luck* (I. 15, 25, 27, 34, 41; II. 66). And there are still other ways of expressing the workings of chance. One is with *acertar a* (to happen to): II. 5, 7, 15, 20, 31, 35. Another is "so might the dice roll" (I. 25). Sometimes it

The following are Don Quixote's principal adventures in Part II, which we shall treat more briefly: "The Parliament of Death" (chap. 11), the Knight of the Wood (chap. 14), the lions (chap. 17), the Cave of Montesinos (chap. 22), Master Peter's puppet show (chap. 26), the enchanted boat (chap. 29), Clavileño (chap. 41), the battle with Tosilos (chap. 56), the bulls (chap. 58), and the Knight of the White Moon (chap. 64).

Like the adventure of the fulling mills, those of "The Parliament of Death" and the lions only appear to be ad-

---

is not mere luck that influences events, but "the current of the stars" (I. 27), "the bad influence of the stars" (I. 52), "the determination of the spheres" (II. 7), "just and favorable disposition of Heaven" (I. 36).

Careful examination in context of the above references and of many others not listed reveals several interesting things. First, the linguistic evidence of the operation of chance, fortune, providence, and the influence of the stars diminishes visibly in Part II and particularly in those many chapters where the lives of Don Quixote and Sancho are dominated by the practical jokes and sham adventures contrived by the Duke and Duchess. Second, Cervantes (or Benengeli) as narrator tends to use *luck, happen to,* and like means to express the influence of extrahuman powers on events. Only in relating Don Quixote's death at the end of Part II does he bring in the *possibility* of heavenly intervention: "because, either on account of the melancholy brought on by seeing himself defeated, or by the disposition of Heaven that ordered it so, he was taken with a fever" (II. 74). On the other hand, a number of characters are prone to distinguish between chance and providence. For example, when Fernando is begged to take Dorotea to wife, he is asked to consider "that not by chance, as it seemed, but by the particular providence of Heaven had all those people met in a place where none expected to" (I. 36). The Captive Captain sometimes likes to think that his luck was rendered good by Heaven's will: "and luck willed, which might have been bad if Heaven had not ordained otherwise" (I. 41). Near the end of Part II Don Quixote likewise distinguished between fortune and providence. As he and Sancho sadly discuss his last defeat, he says: "What I can tell you is that there is no fortune in the world, nor do the things occurring there, whether good or bad, happen by chance but rather by the particular providence of Heaven; hence what is often said: each of us is the forger of his fortune. I have forged mine but not with the necessary prudence" (II. 66). Despite the oft-recognized ambiguity of part of the knight's speech, there is not the slightest doubt that he is assuming full responsibility for his crucial defeat. And this becomes him, for he has amply demonstrated that he belongs to the small and heroic company of those who are not content to be creatures of circumstance, but who dare to try to be what they have chosen to be.

ventures. The first is quickly recognized as a wagonload of actors costumed to play "The Parliament of Death." The second provides Don Quixote with an occasion to demonstrate courage in the presence of real lions; only the lions are not fully cooperative. The adventures of the Knight of the Wood, the bulls, and the Knight of the White Moon are born of a desire to exalt the beauty of a lady. In this they resemble the adventure of the merchants from Toledo. The adventures of the puppet show, the enchanted boat, Clavileño, and the battle with Tosilos are all undertaken to help people in distress. In his defense of books of chivalry (I. 50) Don Quixote presents as a typical knightly undertaking the improvised tale of the Knight of the Lake. The adventure of the Cave of Montesinos is a personal realization of that kind of descent into nether regions perhaps pregnant with chivalrous possibilities. What happens in the Cave of Montesinos is a dream. It has this in common with the adventure of the wineskins.

As can readily be seen, Don Quixote reveals about the same motives and intentions in these adventures as in those of Part I. But there are sufficient differences between the two groups to warrant analyzing them somewhat differently. It will be instructive to begin by noting some of these differences.

Only one of the adventures in Part II depends on gross misinterpretation of visible reality: the enchanted boat. Don Quixote sees the lions for what they are. If he takes the puppet show for real life, it is partly because he falls under the immediate spell of artistic illusion. This is several degrees removed from taking windmills for giants. And there are four adventures which Don Quixote doesn't initiate at all. They look perfectly authentic because they were contrived to look so by people who had already read Part I. The contrived adventures are: the Knight of the Wood, Clavileño, the battle with Tosilos, and the Knight of the White

Moon.[7] In these Don Quixote's book-born madness no longer plays freely over the circumstances of chance encounter. Moreover, it is difficult here to think of a "doctrine of error" operating to make Don Quixote responsible for his mistakes. A brief review of these adventures will suffice to reveal their nature.

With the approval of the Barber and the Priest, Sansón Carrasco sets out on Don Quixote's trail. His purpose is to defeat Don Quixote in battle and require him to return home, where he may be restored to sanity. In other words, he is to be the instrument of Don Quixote's cure. In due time he does overtake Don Quixote and engages him in battle. But his horse, like Rocinante and the Basque's mule on former occasions, proves undependable at a critical moment in the battle, and Carrasco is brought to the ground with a jolt. When he is alone with his squire, the squire suggests that if they don't go home now, they deserve to be considered as crazy as Don Quixote. To which Carrasco answers, "it is idle to think that I shall return home before I have thrashed Don Quixote; and I shall not be led to seek him now by the desire that he regain his sanity but rather by that of vengeance" (II. 15). As was apparent in the adventure of the galley slaves, in the world of *Don Quixote* no characters are solely instruments. None is made to wear so tight a mission as to stifle the expression of his inner impulses. Carrasco is free to indulge his own folly and to fall prisoner to his own emotions. In the end, as the Knight of the White Moon, he defeats Don Quixote and sends him home.

The adventure of Clavileño was contrived by the Duke and Duchess for their own amusement. It is in the nature of

7. This list by no means covers all the episodes that arise out of the premeditated intervention of such characters as Sansón Carrasco, the Duke and Duchess, and Don Antonio Moreno. A goodly portion of what happens in Part II comes about as a result of their contrivances, and these contrivances probably account in part for the reduced operation of chance in Part II.

an elaborate practical joke. By the terms of their invention, Don Quixote is allowed to achieve this adventure at minimum physical cost: singed whiskers and a short fall when Clavileño is exploded. Doña Rodríguez truly believes in Don Quixote's mission and implores him to be the champion of her seduced daughter. The Duke and Duchess see entertainment value in the situation and try to shape it to that end. Since the real seducer has fled the country, they assign one of their lackeys to his place on the day of the joust. Before the battle begins, the lackey spies the afflicted damsel, falls in love with her, and declares himself defeated and ready to marry her. This defrauds the Duke of the pleasure of witnessing a much anticipated spectacle and offers Don Quixote the satisfaction of believing that he has righted a wrong. After Don Quixote leaves the ducal palace, the Duke unloads his disappointment and anger on the bare back of his amorous servant.

Looking at these adventures with reference to those who contrived them, we may note that each pair of adventures turns out quite differently than was intended, and that the subsequent conduct of the intender is modified by unforeseen emotions. As for Don Quixote, he tastes victory thrice and is vanquished once. Can either the victories or the defeat be ascribed to the accuracy or inaccuracy of his interpretation of reality or to the workings of inexorable moral law?

If we were to classify Don Quixote's successes and failures in Part II on the same basis as we did those of Part I, the list would be as follows: four successes (Knight of the Wood, lions, Clavileño, Tosilos); five failures ("The Parliament of Death," puppet show, enchanted boat, bulls, Knight of the White Moon); and one adventure which must be called ambiguous (Cave of Montesinos). According to this list, Don Quixote is more successful in Part II than in Part I. If we look at the adventures in the light of Don Quixote's responsibility for what happens, we must remember that four of them are contrived and thus not principally his responsibility. If for the moment we exclude from consideration the adventures not initiated by Don Quixote, we may then say that he is less successful in Part II than in Part I. Furthermore, and despite the success of three of the contrived adventures, it is clear that in Part II Don Quixote's spirit is enveloped ever more frequently by the dark clouds of dejection. In a later chapter we shall consider whether the sham adventures and the dejection are in some way related.

The purpose of the preceding pages is not to suggest that human beings are held to no responsibility for their actions and their destinies in the world of *Don Quixote*. It is rather to demonstrate that what goes on there cannot be fully understood as an expression of moral law. If we look at *Don Quixote* for reflections of Cervantes the moralist, we do indeed find that he tends to punish his characters for their mistakes. If, on the other hand, we view *Don Quixote* as a world created by an artist, we see that it is altogether too spacious and complex to be adequately represented by ethical formula.

We began our examination of the adventures with the notion that those of Part I are the product of chance encounter and bookish recollection. We accepted the opinion that to a degree their outcome is governed by a kind of doctrine of error. Nevertheless, after classifying them according to success and failure, we found it impossible to adjust them fully to any discoverable moral order. We concluded that this could be explained in part by the operation of chance and in part by the interplay of stubbornly independent lives. By "stubbornly independent lives" I mean those that are refractory to externally imposed roles or missions. When the trajectories of such lives cross, what ethical formula can embrace all the motives, intentions, actions, and reactions so brought together?

All that we have said about the adventures of Part I can

be said also about those of Part II, but we must add that the latter show even more clearly the incalculable effects of interacting lives moving among the shadows of illusion and reality. In Part I the course of Don Quixote's life is determined in large part by the clash of his book-inspired motives and intentions with outward circumstance and with the spontaneous and alien reactions of the people he happens to meet. In Part II his book-born madness has to contend also with the calculated schemes (and incalculable effects) of those who know him well or have read the published record of his earlier adventures. We may thus conclude that in Part II as in Part I the interplay of literature and life is one of the conditions of living in the created world of *Don Quixote*. What differences there are may be attributed largely to the fact that in Part II literature is doubly refracted through human minds and wills.

As yet we have by no means exhausted the light which the study of Don Quixote's adventures may shed on the world where they occur. If read aright, they have much to suggest about the nature of reality in that world. To find out what this is, we must review some of them in greater detail than we have already done.

When Don Quixote first set out upon the roads of Spain to fulfill his knightly mission, he had no squire. On his first three adventures (muleteers, Andrés, merchants from Toledo), he was accompanied only by the ideas and ideals he had acquired from his reading of chivalric literature. These helped him shape what he saw to his fancy, and so he was able to take wanton wenches for high-born maidens, inns for castles, a rich farmer and six merchants for knights. Having no squire at his side, he did not share his experience of these people and things with a sympathetic companion, nor examine it in friendly conversation. If these adventures suggest anything about the nature of reality, it is that at a given moment in their existence people and things may allow more uses than their past ever seemed to promise. As an example of this, we may recall that the wenches did minister to Don Quixote's needs and attend him at his knighting just as they might have done had they been the illustrious ladies of his imagination.

The first adventure that Don Quixote encountered after taking a squire is that of the windmills. As knight and squire were riding along the plain, Don Quixote called to Sancho's attention some thirty or forty giants with whom he meant to do battle. Sancho at once recognized the giants as windmills and informed his master of this fact. But so full was Don Quixote's head of encounters between giants and knights that he was unable to heed Sancho's warning. As we know, he attacked the giants and was defeated. In this adventure we see one of the abundant examples of Don Quixote's misinterpretations of reality. Sancho knew the giants were windmills. Only Don Quixote could have made so ridiculous a mistake as to believe them giants.

The adventure with the Basque started when Don Quixote took two monks of the order of St. Benedict for evil enchanters carrying off in a coach a princess whom they had stolen. On hearing that his master intended to save her, Sancho declared the true identity of the monks and ventured the opinion that this affair would be worse than that of the windmills. Despite such evidence of good sight and good sense, Sancho tried to collect the first spoils of battle from the first monk who fell to earth, and later, at the moment of Don Quixote's victory over the Basque, he dropped to his knees and asked his master for the island he supposed now won.

The adventure of the two flocks of sheep began when Don Quixote spied down the road a large cloud of dust drifting in their direction. Don Quixote pointed it out to Sancho and told him that it was a large army recruited from many nations. This time Sancho did not at once contradict his master. Rather did he remark that two armies were taking the field, since a similar cloud of dust could be seen approaching from the opposite direction. No doubt the reader remembers the knight's fantastic description of the make-up of the opposing armies and of the motive of their quarrel. He may remember too the squire's credulous and fascinated interest in the imminent battle. Only too late, when his master was charging into the fray, did Sancho realize that the contending armies were really two flocks of sheep. One difference between this adventure and the preceding one is that in the adventure of the windmills only Don Quixote could have misinterpreted the reality before him, whereas in that of the two flocks of sheep almost anyone might have misinterpreted it, although probably not for so long a time nor in the same way as did Don Quixote.

The adventure of the dead body occurred at night. As master and man were riding along their dark and lonely way, they saw approaching from afar a great number of mysterious lights. As knight and squire watched, they perceived that the lights were torches carried by about twenty white-shirted figures on horseback, followed by a litter covered with mourning and by six other riders dressed in black to the very feet of their mules. This vision was weird enough to have puzzled anybody. Don Quixote, uncertain how to interpret it, called on the procession to halt and give an account of itself. Receiving no satisfactory answer, he laid about him with his lance and put to rout all but one unfortunate fellow whose mule had fallen on him and broken his leg. From the injured man he learned that the procession consisted of priests taking a dead man to Segovia for burial. Once more Don Quixote misinterprets reality, but here, more than in earlier adventures, circumstances inclined him to error. And hard-headed Sancho was able to lift no warning voice. It is interesting to note that the white-shirted figures misinterpret Don Quixote just as badly as he does them: they take him for a demon from hell.

After the adventure of the dead body, squire and knight turned off the road and into a small mountain valley, which they ascended in search of water. They had not gone far when they heard a roaring as of water falling from some great height. Continuing to advance, they began to hear the sound of measured blows accompanied by the rattling of iron chains. The fearsome din of rushing water, ponderous blows, and rattling chains in a place so dark and solitary would justify the wildest imaginings. Don Quixote and Sancho Panza had no means of arriving at a proper interpretation of it until the light of morning revealed the blows to be the result of the regular fall of fulling hammers operated by water power. Little by little, Cervantes is showing us how difficult it can be to read aright the face of reality. One would not always need to have his head full of chivalric chimeras to wander off the road of reason.

As Don Quixote and Sancho first faced the mysterious night of the adventure just recounted, the former announced somewhat pompously that it was by Heaven's will that he had been born to face such dangers and do such deeds as this night seemed to offer. Throughout the night Sancho suffered the agony of fear. The contrast between what both had felt and the reality that appeared before them with the dawn set them off in gales of laughter, and Sancho even dared to mock his master's pompous words. This brought him a couple of smart blows from the knight's lance and caused his gaiety to vanish. Such recent experience did not incline Sancho to extravagant misinterpretation of reality as he and his master rode along that morning in a light rain, and Don Quixote thought he saw a mounted man approaching them with Mambrino's helmet on his head. The reader is promptly informed that the helmet is really a barber's basin worn over a new hat to protect it from the rain. From a distance Sancho would only concede that the approaching rider wore a shiny object on his head. When he finally got it in his hands, he recognized it immediately for what it was, and only under duress would he ever call it a helmet.

When Don Quixote and Sancho met the chain of galley slaves, Sancho was able at once to identify them for his master and to warn him that they were not wronged men but criminals punished for their crimes. Of course, for Don Quixote they remained men deprived, perhaps unjustly, of their freedom. In the heat of battle Sancho helped to free Ginés de Pasamonte, the boldest of the lot. But when the fracas was over, Sancho quickly recovered his good sense and led his master away from the wrath of the Holy Brotherhood and into the comparative safety of the Sierra Morena.

In the adventure of the wineskins Don Quixote arose from his bed dreaming that he was fighting the dread giant Pandafilando. Blindly he slashed about his room with his naked sword and cut up some wineskins full of red wine. Sancho reported the action to the other guests at the inn as a battle between his master and a giant. Despite the innkeeper's rueful guess that his wineskins were the victims of Don Quixote's anger, Sancho stoutly maintained that he had seen the severed head and spurting blood. In this adventure Don Quixote's irrational behavior has a rational explanation: his dream. Only sensible Sancho can fairly be charged with misinterpreting reality.

In the adventure of the penitents Don Quixote saw a procession of men carrying an image of the Virgin Mary dressed in mourning. Taking the image for a noble lady abducted by villainous scoundrels, Don Quixote prepared to rescue her. The Barber, the Priest, the Canon from Toledo, and Sancho all tried to restrain him. Sancho told him quite exactly what the procession was and warned that he was assaulting their Catholic faith, but to no avail. Once more Don Quixote is alone in his gross misinterpretation of reality. And this is the last adventure of Part I. For our present purpose those of Part II are irrelevant.[8]

The adventures summarized above reveal a gamut of misinterpretations of reality leading from those which only Don Quixote could have made to those which almost anyone might have made. That Don Quixote should often misinterpret reality is not surprising because he is mad and, as Sancho once remarked to himself, "of a madness that most often takes one thing for another, and judges white to be black and black to be white, as was apparent when he said that the windmills were giants, and the friars' mules dromedaries, and the flocks of sheep hostile armies, and many other things of this sort" (II. 10). How about Sancho? He recognized the windmills, the barber's basin, and the penitents for what they were, and from them he stood aloof. The friars on mules the size of dromedaries and the galley slaves he also recognized at once, but in these adventures

---

8. Analysis of the adventures in Part II would shed no new light on our inquiry into the nature of reality in *Don Quixote*. As previously noted, four of the adventures were deliberately contrived so as to be accepted as knightly adventures. As for "The Parliament of Death," neither Sancho nor his master recognized the costumed players until they identified themselves. There was never any question about the lions being lions, but only whether it was prudent to offer to fight them. Sancho didn't believe Don Quixote's account of what he claimed to have seen in the Cave of Montesinos, but in this adventure there is no reality except that of Don Quixote's dream; that is to say, master and man did not disagree about a reality which they had equal opportunity to observe. In the puppet show, Don Quixote was carried away by the excitement of the storied chase. He went into action before there could be any discussion, and in the end he confessed his error. The adventure of the bulls was likewise consummated too rapidly for discussion, and at the last Don Quixote recognized the bulls as bulls. In other words, all but one of the adventures in Part II fail to evoke conflicting interpretations of visible reality. The exception is the adventure of the enchanted boat: Don Quixote and Sancho disagree about the water mills of Part II as they had about the windmills of Part I.

such recognition did not keep him from participating in them. He briefly accepted the two flocks of sheep as armies. He could make no sense at all of the appearances presented by the adventures of the dead body, the fulling mills, and the wineskins. Unquestionably, some of Sancho's reactions to the realities he has to face have more to do with Sancho's nature than with the nature of these realities or the way they present themselves. Of this we shall have more to say later. Here it is fair to remark that some of Sancho's reactions do also suggest that the interpretation of reality may sometimes be a thorny question. Even his mad master came to realize how problematical it might be. Witness the words he spoke during the adventure of "The Parliament of Death": "On the faith of a knight-errant . . . when I first saw this cart I imagined that some great adventure was offering itself to me; but now I say that it is necessary to touch appearances with one's hand to be disabused" (II. 11).[9] Little by little, observation carries us from the spectacle of madness unable to discriminate windmills from giants to the realization that in the world of *Don Quixote* reality is often puzzling and that one of its most important characteristics is its susceptibility to varied interpretation.[10]

9. This is not the only occasion that prompts Don Quixote to apply to reality the test of palpability. The phrase he uses most often is *tocar con la mano* (to touch with one's hand). See I. 47; II. 11, 14, 23, 36. The reader may remember that one reason for Sancho's refusal to believe that he was tossed in a blanket by enchantment was that it was a palpable experience. Other examples of *tocar con la mano* may be found in I. 48, 50; II. 1, 9.

10. In the following chapters on enchantment, reality, and illusions, the reader may contemplate further evidence of the quixotic world's susceptibility to varied interpretation and man's propensity to discover in that world whatever seems to fulfill the expectations carried in his head. Before beginning those chapters, the reader may find it rewarding to sample three or four contemporary viewpoints on such matters. They suggest that Cervantes anticipated artistically some of the formulations of twentieth-century thinkers.

The first viewpoint comes from Karl Britton, *Communication. A Philosophical Study of Language* (New York, 1939). It claims that facts are not the simple, inevitable things that Don Quixote's mockers may have believed: "We cannot define a fact except by reference to the meaning of a statement (or to some other form of learned discriminating selective response). To the same events an infinite variety of responses is possible: he who understands 'p' makes only certain responses and not others. It is this that *introduces* limitation, structure; *events as such have no structure.* . . . A world without minds is a world without structure, without relations and qualities, *without facts*" (pp. 205-206).

The next viewpoints are taken from E. H. Gombrich, *Art and Illusion* (New York, 1960). They have to do with "mental set," something clearly present in Don Quixote. Here is the first: "All culture and all communication depend on the interplay between expectation and observation, the waves of fulfillment, disappointment, right guesses, and wrong moves that make up our daily life" (p. 60). The second: "What we call 'mental set' may be precisely that state of readiness to start projecting, to thrust out the tentacles of phantom colors and phantom images which always flicker around our perceptions" (p. 227). And the third: "There is no reality without interpretation; just as there is no innocent eye, there is no innocent ear" (p. 363).

3 · ENCHANTMENT

*E*NCHANTMENT HEADS the list of the book-acquired elements of chivalry which filled Don Quixote's fantasy: "His fantasy was filled with all that he read in books, enchantment as well as quarrels, battles, challenges, wounds, courtings, loves, torments, and impossible nonsense; and so fixed did it become in his mind that the whole apparatus of fabulous inventions which he read was true, that for him there was in the world no history more authentic" (I. 1). Being so familiar with the operation of enchantment in the romances of chivalry and believing in it so firmly, it is not surprising that Don Quixote found much evidence of it in the real world around him. But he is not the only one to find it, and there are many who talk about it in one connection or another. In fact, it is so prevalent in the world of *Don Quixote*, one is forced to conclude that it is a major feature of that world. We shall therefore attempt to survey its operation and to interpret its meaning, considering it first in relation to Don Quixote.

As Don Quixote makes his first sally, he dreams of the day when a sage will record for posterity the history of his famous deeds (I. 2). Before he makes his final sally, he learns that his dream has come true. The sage is now called an enchanter (II. 2, 3). Before he makes his second sally, the hostile enchanter Freston carries off his library: books, room, and all (I. 7). Just prior to the battle with the Basque, Don Quixote takes two black-robed Benedictine friars for enchanters. During both sojourns at Juan Palomeque's inn, a variety of painful and puzzling events occur. First, the pitiless melee touched off by Don Quixote's interception of Maritornes' nocturnal visit to the muleteer (I. 16); then,

Sancho's inability to escape being tossed in a blanket, and Don Quixote's inability to come to his rescue (I. 17); then, Don Quixote's night-long suspension by the wrist (I. 43); then, the general fight over the question of the barber's basin and a packsaddle (I. 45); and finally, the knight's removal from the inn in an oxcart (I. 46). Between the two stays at the inn a friendly enchanter whisks Sancho from Sierra Morena to El Toboso and back with uncommon speed (I. 31). The little boat which carried master and man almost to a watery grave is supplied by enchanters (II. 29). And who but enchanters could have scratched Don Quixote's face so painfully in the middle of the night (II. 46), or put up the green nets in the woods to entangle him (II. 58), or built the talking head which he had heard in Barcelona (II. 62)?

There is much more evidence of enchantment in the life of Don Quixote than the thirteen instances listed above, but with these we may begin our attempt at interpretation. One of the first and most obvious things about them is that they represent the apparent fulfillment of Don Quixote's book-inspired expectations, or an explanation of phenomena otherwise difficult to explain, or a combination of both. For example, Don Quixote had often read of sages who wrote the histories of the knights they favored. Hence the publication of his adventures was the fulfillment of a confident expectation. If Sancho wondered how their historian could report what they did and said in solitude, his master could easily explain it by affirming that their historian was an enchanter of the kind to whom all things are revealed (II. 2). Since Don Quixote expected to meet enchanters face to face, it was easy for him to take the black-robed friars as such. Being aware that enchanters often provided rapid transportation for the knights they served, Don Quixote had no trouble in explaining Sancho's swift trip to El Toboso or the presence of the enchanted boat on the bank of the river Ebro. In the rest of the instances already cited, enchantment tends more to explanation than to fulfillment. Don Quixote's niece suggests enchantment to him as an explanation for the disappearance of his library. In the other cases enchantment is his own explanation.

While some of the episodes alluded to above may be profitably examined in the light of Don Quixote's most intimate reaction to them, for now we shall merely consider them from the point of view of their relation to objective reality. Let us consider what it was in the world about him that allowed Don Quixote to turn so often to enchantment.

Don Quixote took the black-robed Benedictine friars for enchanters, because they appeared to be part of a total situation resembling those which in the romances of chivalry frequently produced adventures involving evil enchanters. But Sancho was not deceived. Probably only a man mad with Don Quixote's peculiar madness could conjure up enchanters with such a slight real basis. The other examples, however, tend to supply a more substantial basis in reality. Don Quixote never sees the published account of his first two sallies from home, but the evidence for its existence is abundant and thoroughly convincing. Neither does he see Freston carry off his library, but the library does disappear. There is no doubt that all-embracing discord twice erupts at the inn, that Don Quixote cannot rescue Sancho from being tossed in a blanket, that he is hung up by the wrist, and that he is removed in a cage on an oxcart. Sancho really does return from a trip sooner than Rocinante's speed and endurance would allow; a little boat is actually found on the riverbank; Don Quixote's face is scratched mysteriously in the middle of the night; such green nets as are not usually found in the forest are really hanging there; and real words do issue from the mouth of the artificial head.

The reader knows how to explain all of these mysterious and generally painful happenings attributed by Don Quixote to enchantment. He knows they spring directly from the knight's madness or from the folly or contrivance of others or from the operation of chance. But Don Quixote never discovers the true cause of any but the green nets, which were hung in the trees to trap little birds. Furthermore, it is doubtful if anyone, no matter how sane, would have been able to provide rational explanations for all of them.[1] On the basis of such instances as these, we may be tempted to regard enchantment as a gauge whose needle wavers between Don Quixote's madness and the labyrinthine nature of the world.

While Don Quixote finds enchanters meddling in his affairs in a variety of ways, they do seem to have a specialty: to change the appearance of one person or thing into that of another. Following is a reasonably complete list of these changes: giants are changed into windmills (I. 8); armies are converted into sheep (I. 18); Mambrino's helmet looks exactly like a barber's basin (I. 25, 45); and a horse's fine trappings like a donkey's rude packsaddle (I. 44, 45); the Princess Micomicona threatens to become Dorotea (I. 37, 46); Dulcinea is transformed into a coarse peasant wench (II. 8, 10); an enemy enchanter assumes Don Quixote's figure and allows himself to be defeated by the Knight of the Wood (II. 14); the Knight of the Wood turns into Sansón Carrasco (II. 14, 16); certain historical and legendary figures become puppets (II. 26); the Countess Trifaldi appears to wear the face of the Duke's majordomo (II. 44); the seducer of Doña Rodríguez' daughter takes on the appearance of the lackey Tosilos (II. 56, 66, 67).

With the exception of two examples, the transformations

1. The narrator expresses this attitude in connection with the episode of the enchanted head: "and except for Don Antonio's two friends, no other person knew the secret of the enchantment, and if Don Antonio had not first revealed it to his friends, they too would have been as astonished as the rest; for it was impossible not to be impressed by a thing so cunningly contrived" (II. 62).

listed above fall naturally into two groups. In the first group, Don Quixote has to transform reality before there is anything for the enchanters to do; in the second, Don Quixote shows no initiative in the metamorphoses that must precede the work of enchantment. The first group consists of windmills, sheep, barber's basin, and packsaddle. Only after Don Quixote's mad fantasy has converted these prosaic things into giants, armies, Mambrino's helmet, and equine trappings, is there scope for the operation of enchantment. The two odd examples are the enchantment of Dulcinea and the deceit of the enemy enchanter mentioned by Sansón Carrasco, alias the Knight of the Wood. The enchanted Dulcinea, whom Sancho presents to his master in the form of a coarse peasant girl, really is a coarse peasant girl. Enchantment cannot restore her to the being she never possessed. As for the enemy enchanter, he never appears. He is merely a figment of Carrasco's imagination. Our second group is composed of the Princess Micomicona, the Knight of the Wood, the historical and legendary figures, the Countess Trifaldi, and the seducer of Doña Rodríguez' daughter. Except for the figures in Master Peter's puppet show, who owe their illusion of vital reality to the power of art, all the rest are the creatures of do-gooders and pranksters. In Don Quixote's view it is the intervention of malicious enchanters that threatens to convert Micomicona into Dorotea, the Knight of the Wood into Sansón Carrasco, the Countess Trifaldi into the majordomo, and the seducer into Tosilos. Both groups suggest that the transformations attributed by Don Quixote to enchantment might better be called restorations. There is much to be said, then, for the notion that enchantment is the principle by which Don Quixote accounts for the (to him) disturbing fact that people and things so often assume the appearance of what they are.

Unlike Don Quixote, Sancho did not embark on his

chivalric career with his head full of bookish notions of enchantment. Nevertheless, enchantment touched his life almost as often as it did his master's. What it did to him and how he reacted to it merit study.

Sancho was sleeping peacefully in the starry garret of the inn when Maritornes jumped into his bed to escape detection by her master. In the ensuing general scuffle Sancho received as many hard knocks as anybody and with even less knowledge of their origin. In the darkness of the brief calm which followed the storm, Don Quixote asked him if he was asleep. With understandable irritation Sancho replied, "How am I to sleep, confound it . . . when it seems only that all the devils have been at me tonight" (I. 17). As we have already remarked, Don Quixote explained the mysterious hubbub as the work of an enchanted Moor, and this explanation appeared to satisfy Sancho, particularly after the officer of the Holy Brotherhood came back and smashed a lamp on Don Quixote's head. Here is Sancho's final comment: "No doubt, sir, this is the enchanted Moor . . . and he must be keeping the treasure for others, and for us only the punches and lamp blows" (I. 17).

This is Sancho's first encounter with enchantment. If he accepts enchantment, it is probably because no other explanation for what has happened to him comes to mind. In any case, it appears that he is not yet ready to accept enchantment as a universal explanation for the ills that befall him. On the morning after the episode just mentioned, Sancho is tossed in a blanket. As we know, Don Quixote explains this, too, by enchantment. Sancho comments: "It's my opinion that those who made sport with me were not phantoms or enchanted men, as your worship says, but men of flesh and blood like us; and they all had names as I heard when they were tossing me" (I. 18). Much later Don Quixote tries again to persuade Sancho that he was tossed in a blanket by enchanted men, and once more Sancho rejects the explanation (I. 46). He rejects it because in his eyes there is nothing mysterious about the episode: it occurred in broad daylight, those who tossed him were palpable men, they were identified by name. As yet Sancho has no inner need for enchantment.

While most of the guests at the inn were attending the reading of *The Man Too Curious for His Own Good*, Don Quixote arose from his bed dreaming that he was fighting the dread giant Pandafilando. Blindly he slashed about his room with his naked sword and cut up some wine-skins full of red wine. Sancho reported the fracas to the other guests at the inn as a battle between his master and a giant. Despite the innkeeper's rueful guess that his wine-skins were the victims of Don Quixote's wrath, Sancho stoutly maintained that he had seen the severed head and gushing blood. All repaired to the knight's room, and Sancho searched in vain for the giant's head. His comment was: "I already know that everything about this house is enchanted, because the last time, in this very same place, I received many punches and blows without knowing who gave them to me nor ever seeing a soul; and now the head that I saw cut off with my very own eyes doesn't appear nor the blood that flowed from the body like a fountain" (I. 35). Sancho's third brush with enchantment seems more like the second than the first. The perforated wineskins are clearly visible and have been correctly identified in Sancho's presence. Why, then, is Sancho unable to see things as they are? Lest we miss the point, the narrator tells us: "And Sancho awake was worse than his master asleep, so possessed was he by the promises his master had made him" (I. 35). If the giant is dead, Sancho may expect his promised reward. For the first time, Sancho needs enchantment to defend his illusions.

As we have already seen, there was a second general fracas at the inn, preceded by two minor quarrels and followed by the Holy Brotherhood's attempt forcibly to arrest Don Quixote. At this point Sancho is moved to exclaim: "By God, what my master says of the enchantments of this castle is true, since it is not possible to live here one hour in peace" (I. 45). Sancho is inclined to turn to the supernatural to explain the unnatural discord which hovers so persistently over the inn, but he is not yet a prisoner of enchantment. He rejects it as an explanation of his master's abduction in a cage. This episode is worth examining, because in it Sancho's attitude has become ambivalent.

The Priest and the Barber want to get Don Quixote back to his village, where they hope he may be restored to sanity. They arrange to carry him off on an oxcart in such a way as to make him think he is enchanted. He accepts his enchantment, but Sancho does not. Even though the perpetrators of the hoax are disguised, Sancho is able to recognize them. The very consideration that rendered Sancho blind to the wineskins opened his eyes to the true nature of Don Quixote's abductors. Note the reproachful words he addressed to the Priest: "Damn the devil. If it wasn't for your reverence, at this very hour my master would be married to the Princess Micomicona, and I would be a count at least, for I could expect no less, both on account of the generosity of my master, the Knight of the Sad Countenance, and of the greatness of my services" (I. 47).

In this episode we see Sancho rejecting a particular instance of enchantment while accepting enchantment in general. We may note also that he feels a need to rationalize his position. To do this, he must compare Don Quixote's supposedly enchanted behavior with the behavior of people really enchanted. But where is Sancho to find a standard of comparison? When Don Quixote first asked him what he thought of this new enchantment, Sancho admitted he was not well read in "errant writings" (I. 47). The following words addressed to the Priest, the Barber, and the Canon

43

show where Sancho found his standard: "Now, gentlemen, whether you like me or not for what I say, the fact of the matter is that my lord Don Quixote is just as enchanted as my mother; he has all his wits, he eats and drinks and takes care of his bodily needs, just like he did yesterday before they caged him up. This being so, how do you expect me to believe that he is enchanted? For I've heard many people say that the enchanted neither eat nor sleep nor talk, and my master, if they don't hold him back, will talk more than thirty lawyers" (I. 47).

Obviously, Sancho is using notions of enchantment that have currency beyond the circle of chivalry. The following is another specimen of the reasoning he uses in attempting to persuade his master that he is not enchanted: "Can you deny what is commonly said everywhere when a person is out of sorts: 'I don't know what's the matter with so and so. He neither eats nor drinks nor sleeps nor answers sensibly what he's asked; indeed he seems enchanted.' From which you may gather that those who neither eat nor drink nor sleep nor satisfy the natural urges I mention are enchanted; but not those who feel the urge your worship does and who drink when they can and eat when they have something to eat and answer everything they are asked" (I. 49).[2]

In the adventure of the penitents, which occurs shortly after Sancho has made the remarks quoted above, one of the penitents knocks Don Quixote from his horse with a stout pole. As the knight lies senseless on the ground, Sancho runs up and calls out to the penitent not to strike again, for his master is a poor enchanted knight who has never harmed a soul (I. 52). If it seems paradoxical for Sancho to call his master enchanted when he has so recently tried to convince him that he is not, the paradox is easily explained. The

2. Don Quixote readily agrees with Sancho that enchanted people are usually thought of as not eating, drinking, or sleeping. Later, he confirms this notion on the basis of his experience in the Cave of Montesinos (II. 23).

penitents know nothing about Don Quixote except that he has attacked them without any motive understandable to them. To save his master from their justifiable wrath, Sancho must try to relieve him of responsibility for his unreasonable attack. To do this, he appeals to the same widely recognized notion of enchantment that he has just used in arguing with his master. In effect, he says: "Don't beat my master. He is under some kind of spell and should not be blamed for what he cannot help." Before we continue our survey of Sancho's involvement with enchantment, perhaps we should pause to inquire whether there are other characters who also appeal to a kind of enchantment not necessarily related to knight-errantry.

Just before the adventure of the penitents, Don Quixote and his companions meet a goatherd. The goatherd tells them the story of the beautiful Leandra who disdained her local suitors for a flashy soldier just back from foreign wars. The rejected suitors wander off into a kind of desperate Arcadia, where "Echo repeats the name of Leandra wherever it can sound: Leandra resounds in the woodlands, the brooks murmur Leandra, and Leandra keeps us all in suspense and enchanted, hoping without hope and fearing without knowing what we fear" (I. 51).

Another example of enchantment which agrees very well with Sancho's notions is found in the traveling student's description of Basilio's state after learning that he was about to lose his beloved Quiteria:

> From the moment Basilio learned that the beautiful Quiteria was to marry Camacho the rich, he has never more been heard to laugh or make a sensible remark, and he goes about ever pensive and sad, talking to himself and showing clear signs of having lost his mind. He eats and sleeps little, and what he eats is fruit, and when he does sleep, it's in the open air and on the hard ground like a

45

brute animal. From time to time he looks at the sky, and at other times he fixes his gaze on the ground with such an air of enchantment that he looks like a clothed statue whose garments are moved by the wind [II. 30].

Is it not clear that in the world of *Don Quixote* enchantment extends beyond the projection of Don Quixote's madness? In the form in which we have just seen it, enchantment is a part of common human experience.[3]

Several days before Don Quixote and Sancho make their final sally, Sancho orders his wife to get his donkey in good shape for the road. He tells her of the many dangers they expect to confront, and ends up with these words: "And all this would be flowers of lavender if we didn't have to deal with Yanguesans and enchanted Moors" (II. 5). These are prophetic words. In Part II enchanters and enchantment are going to give Sancho much more to do than they did in Part I. The experiences he has with them fall naturally into three groups.

Let us consider the smallest group. When Don Quixote overcomes the Knight of the Wood, Sancho expresses some doubts as to whether it is enchantment that causes the defeated knight and his squire to look exactly like Sansón Carrasco and Tomé Cecial (II. 16). When Sancho notices that the Duke's majordomo wears the face of the Countess Trifaldi, he again voices reservations regarding his master's usual explanation (II. 44). Neither of these apparent transformations threatens anything important to Sancho. Nothing blinds him to the familiar appearance of these figures.

The second group of experiences shows Sancho trying to use enchantment for his own purposes. Two of the cases in this group may be treated very briefly. Immediately before Don Quixote undertakes the adventure of the lions, he asks

3. Ortega y Gasset suggests for giants the same kind of existence as is here suggested for enchanters and enchantment. See his "Meditaciones del Quijote," in *Obras de José Ortega y Gasset* (Madrid, 1932), p. 69.

Sancho for his helmet without knowing that Sancho has ill-advisedly filled it with newly bought curds. Don Quixote slaps his helmet on his head and is of course much annoyed at the resulting mess. To escape punishment, Sancho tries to shift responsibility for the misplaced curds to enchanters (II. 17). After his ride on Clavileño, Sancho appeals to enchantment to account for the improbabilities of his celestial vision (II. 41).

The remaining example of this kind of enchantment is of greater interest and more consequence. After their failure to find Dulcinea's residence at midnight in El Toboso, Don Quixote sends Sancho back to the village by daylight to find and speak to Dulcinea. Realizing that his mission is an impossible one, Sancho sits down against a tree to seek a solution to his problem. Aware that his master often takes one thing for another, he decides to make him believe that the first girl they meet is Dulcinea. This he succeeds in doing with great ease (II. 10). As anticipated, Don Quixote attributes the disappointing appearance of Dulcinea to the work of envious enchanters. This piece of enchantment engineered by Sancho takes its origin from a deceit practised by Sancho in Sierra Morena, and it will lead to the deception of Sancho himself.

In chapter 31 of Part I Sancho describes the Dulcinea he never really visited as a coarse, ill-smelling peasant girl whom he found winnowing wheat. If he paints her so in his fantastic report, it is partly because his master refuses even to consider marrying the Princess Micomicona. If Sancho can destroy Don Quixote's idealized image of Dulcinea, he may enhance the possibility of a marriage whose consummation would bring him substantial reward. In Part II, as master and man are journeying toward El Toboso, the conversation again touches upon Sancho's alleged earlier visit. When Sancho insists once more that he saw Dulcinea winnowing wheat in a corral, Don Quixote conjectures that this vision of his lady fair can be imputed to the envy of some evil enchanter (II. 8). With this background in mind, Sancho's enchantment of Dulcinea is easily understood. Of course, when Sancho slyly decided to play at enchantment, he didn't know that he would be required to pay for it with 3300 self-inflicted lashes. As the Duchess said, "Good Sancho, intending to play the deceiver, is the deceived" (II. 33).

So far we have reviewed in Part II five cases involving enchantment. Sancho voices some doubt regarding two of them, and thinks himself the instigator of the other three. Seven cases remain. Of them the following leave Sancho relatively unaffected: unable to believe Don Quixote's account of what he saw in the Cave of Montesinos, Sancho supposes that enchanters stuffed his master's head with the nonsense he has just reported (II. 23); to evil enchanters he ascribes the mysterious scratching of Don Quixote's face (II. 51); he supports Don Quixote's opinion that enchanters transformed the seducer of Doña Rodríguez' daughter into the lackey Tosilos (II. 56, 60); he conjectures that the confused Don Alvaro Tarfe is himself enchanted (II. 72). These works of enchantment cost Sancho neither physical pain nor mental anguish. But there are those that do.

In Barcelona harbor Sancho goes aboard a galley. He has never viewed the sea before, nor been aboard a ship. His eyes are already wide with wonder when he is seized by the oarsmen and passed through the air from one end of the ship to the other and back again. So fast is Sancho's wingless flight in these strange surroundings that he can only imagine that all the devils of hell are bearing him off. Before he has recovered from this rough and unsuspected prank, he sees the boatswain give the signal to weigh anchor and then begin to lash the bare backs of the oarsmen. Sancho comments, "These are the things truly enchanted and not the ones my master says. What have these unfortunate fellows done that they flog them so? And how does this single man, who goes whistling to and fro, dare to whip so many people? Now I say this is hell or purgatory at least" (II. 63). Not long after these experiences Don Quixote is conquered by the Knight of the White Moon and compelled to renounce for a year the practice of knighthood. This represents the ebb of Don Quixote's fortunes, but now he explains his defeat not as the work of envious enchanters but as the result of his own weakness. And now it is to sorrowful and dumbfounded Sancho that it all seems a matter of enchantment (II. 64). Before the end of the story Sancho concludes with rueful conviction that there must indeed be evil enchanters. In the incident where Altisidora is supposed to have died for love of Don Quixote, Sancho is martyrized to restore her to life. Sancho can find but one explanation for his strange and painful role in the affair: "Now do I perceive clearly and distinctly that there are enchanters and enchantments in this world, and God save me from them since I cannot save myself" (II. 70).

Sancho and Don Quixote speak of enchantment almost one hundred times. No fewer than fourteen other people refer to it at least once. Most of them do it to placate, humor, or mock Don Quixote. But: the housekeeper appears to believe in it (I. 6); so does the innkeeper (I. 32); and so probably does Teresa Panza (II. 52). Of course these are simple, uneducated folk, but the bright and the educated also come upon days when enchantment seems to offer the only way out. In chapter 50 of Part II the Duchess sends a page with a letter to Sancho's wife Teresa. In addition to the letter, he bears presents and news of her husband, the governor. This is beyond the capacity of the Priest and the Bachelor to believe. They cannot imagine humble Sancho a governor nor Teresa in correspondence with a duchess. How near the Bachelor comes to adopting Don Quixote's usual explanation can be seen in his words: "you still affirm, do you, that the business of Sancho's government is true and that there is a duchess in the world who sends presents and writes letters? Because we don't believe it, even though we have touched the presents and read the letters, and we think that this has to do with our fellow villager Don Quixote, who thinks everything is done by enchantment. And I am inclined to want to touch and feel your worship to see if you are a fantastic ambassador or a man of flesh and blood" (II. 50).

Except for the omission of a few casual references, this is the history of enchantment in *Don Quixote*. There is no doubt Cervantes borrowed it from the romances of chivalry, but with what differences! Perhaps if we compare, even very briefly, enchantment in, say, *Amadis of Gaul* and in *Don Quixote*, it will help us to understand more fully its significance in the latter work.[4]

In *Amadis* enchantment is unthinkable without enchanters. In it there are only two important ones: Urganda the Unknown and Arcalaus. The first is Amadis' friend and protector, the second his enemy. Although they possess supernatural powers and sometimes assume unnatural forms, they do also appear quite often in their own persons and speak directly and audibly to both friends and enemies. Since they are present and active, it is often necessary to try to cope with them. Sometimes this is possible. Nobody questions their effective existence, or regards them as being in any way problematical.

In *Don Quixote* enchantment tends to emanate from anonymous enchanters. It is true that on two occasions Don Quixote invokes the aid of Urganda the Unknown, but

4. Another way of appreciating the richness of the theme of enchantment in *Don Quixote* is to compare Cervantes' use of it with that of Avellaneda in the false *Don Quixote*. As Avellaneda uses it—mechanically and far less frequently than Cervantes—it contributes nothing to the characterization either of reality or of Don Quixote. The latter is a flat character whose views of the world and whose own sanity never become a problem for him. He does not use enchantment to defend his illusion.

she does not respond. It is also true that a number of other known sages and enchanters are called or mentioned: Alquife, Freston, Lirgandeo, and Merlin; but these are either merely remembered names or else disguises in the adventures concocted by Don Quixote's friends and acquaintances. The same may be said of the newly invented Malambruno, and with his name the list of identified enchanters is complete. If there are any effective enchanters in *Don Quixote* beyond the masquerading ones alluded to above, they are nameless, numberless, and invisible. They are dangerous and hard to deal with, and there are those who doubt their very existence. In a word, they are problematical. This is why enchantment seems so mysterious and compels our attention. What can be said, in summary, of enchanters and enchantment?

If enchanters are problematical, enchantment is not. People use it and it has effects. People may use it to relieve themselves of responsibility for certain events or conditions, they may use it to deceive other people, and they may use it as an explanation for whatever they cannot cope with on strictly rational grounds. Two or more of these uses may operate simultaneously. Any attempt to use enchantment deliberately to deceive is likely to produce effects that are incalculable and often unpleasant to the perpetrator. But this is not surprising since one of its attributes is the unpredictability of its effects.

What, then, is enchantment? It can be described in a number of ways. First of all, it is an idea in Don Quixote's head. He found it in literature, he believes in it, he carries it with him into the world of everyday life. For one reason or another the idea is also present in the minds of all the people he meets. Some of them don't believe in it, but on occasion they try to put it to work. In general, it may be said that whether they use it to deceive Don Quixote or Don Quixote uses it to sustain his illusions, it always tends toward the delusion of all concerned. Cervantes has taken pains to point this out, particularly in connection with Sancho, Carrasco, and the Duke and Duchess.

Is there any enchantment in the world which cannot be attributed, directly or indirectly, to Don Quixote's book-inspired madness? We found that Sancho appealed to common human experience to find a standard of enchantment with which to compare his master's supposedly enchanted state, and that both Basilio and Leandra's suitors seemed to be enchanted. In them enchantment is a mental and emotional state which interferes with the normal conduct of their lives, and it does not manifest itself in response to Don Quixote's madness.

Up to this point we have thought of enchantment as being mostly in men's minds. But if it is more than a projection of Don Quixote's madness, if it is really a part of common human experience, how came it there? Is there something in the world itself which propitiates enchantment? On the basis of the foregoing, it would seem that there is something—something inimicable to order and rebellious to reason. As we have observed, life frequently unfolds amidst conflicting purposes sometimes rendered doubly difficult by the operation of chance. And objective reality always remains sufficiently undefined to allow—or invite—multiple interpretation. In a sense, then, enchantment is partly a description of the world.

Many readers have remarked that the world of *Don Quixote* is composed of being *(ser)* and seeming *(parecer)*. Sometimes they speak of a world of being and a world of seeming. To a greater or lesser degree all the characters in *Don Quixote* must live in both these worlds. Defined in terms of its broadest function, enchantment is an artifice created by the human mind confronted with the disconcerting and often painful necessity of reconciling these two worlds.

E HAVE ALREADY examined three fundamental elements of the quixotic world: literature, which is an all-pervasive presence and source of illusions; adventures, which arise from the clash between illusions and reality; and enchantment, which serves to defend illusions against inhospitable reality and perhaps also to characterize that reality. We have also had to concern ourselves with reality, although only incidentally. Now we shall bring it forward and focus our entire attention on it. But it would be well to begin with a little history.

The first person who seriously posed the problem of reality in the works of Cervantes was, if I am not mistaken, Américo Castro. In his *El Pensamiento de Cervantes* he says, "If in Cervantes there is a general preoccupation, prior to all others, it is that of the nature of reality" (p. 79). And also: "Don Quixote is the depository of the theme of fluctuating reality" (p. 80). Since then this attitude of Castro's with regard to the problem of reality has enjoyed an almost general acceptance, and that in spite of the change of point of view expressed by Castro in 1947 in these words: "Some years ago I attempted to interpret *Don Quixote* with excessively occidental criteria, and believed that on occasions Cervantes was interested in determining what reality lay beneath the fluctuation of appearances. But what preoccupies the author is not the problem of truth or of logical error, but of making one feel how reality is always an aspect of the experience of the one who is living it." [1]

In recent years several scholars have again occupied themselves with the problem of reality in *Don Quixote*, among

1. *Miguel de Cervantes Saavedra, Homenaje de Ínsula*, p. 35.

them myself. Writing on the theme, I stated certain conclusions which may be worth citing in part: [2]

If, as far as reality is concerned, there is a distinction generally valid for the entire *Don Quixote*, it is that which separates reality as Cervantes presents it to the reader from reality as the characters of his book see or interpret it. I am going to rest my analysis of the problem on this distinction.

Let the reader, if he will, reconsider, free from the prejudices of other commentaries, the principal adventures of Part I.[3] He will see that there is no motive to doubt the objective reality of windmills, Benedictine friars, Biscayan, Yanguesans, enchanted Moor, flocks of sheep, dead body, fulling mills, etc. Even when the adventures start with mystery, as that of the dead body and that of the fulling mills, Cervantes always ends up telling us exactly what it is about. Even in the prolonged and oft-discussed adventure of Mambrino's helmet, the narrator informs us very early that the helmet is a basin, and there is not even a moment in which anyone, except Don Quixote, believes that it is anything else. I am not going to study these adventures in minutest detail again, because it has already been done in part,[4] and because there is

---

2. The following long quotation and n. 4, 5 and 6 are from my article, "El problema de la realidad en el *Quijote*," *Nueva Revista de Filología Hispánica*, 7 (1953), 490-492.

3. To study the theme of reality, the adventures of Part I seem to me more significant than those of Part II, because most of the latter are adventures which the other characters deliberately create for Don Quixote; that is, they are deceits, and it does not seem probable that Cervantes believed that deliberate deceit revealed anything about objective reality. The adventures of Part II are very important, of course, for the study of illusion and deceit. [We shall see at the end of the chapter that this interpretation allows some rectification.]

4. Cf. A. A. Parker, "El concepto de la verdad en el *Quijote*," *Revista de Filología Española*, 32 (1948), 287-305. I am in agreement with Parker as far as Cervantes' attitude toward reality is concerned, but I cannot completely accept his analysis of the process of deceit nor his interpretation of Don Quixote's character.

another way, not yet made use of, to know whether Cervantes pretended or not to search with the reader for objective reality hidden beneath the fluctuation of appearances.

If the characters of *Don Quixote* are frequently confused or mistaken in the presence of the deceptive appearances of reality, the narrator is not confused nor does he permit the reader to be confused. Besides relating the adventures in such a way that the reader always knows what objective reality is, Cervantes uses several other means to insist on its real nature. For example, long after relating the adventure which occurred in the starry stable of the inn, he alludes again to "that enchanted moor of a muleteer" (I. 43). Although the reader already knows that the moor is the muleteer, the narrator insists upon it again. He does the same in some of his famous recapitulations:

"About that," replied the Bachelor, "there are different opinions, as there are different tastes: some prefer the adventure of the windmills, which to your Grace appeared to be Briareuses and giants; others, that of the fulling mills; this one, the description of the two armies, which later appeared to be two flocks of sheep; that one favors the adventure of the dead body which they were taking to Segovia for burial; one says that the freeing of the galley slaves excels all others; another, that none equals the two Benedictine giants, together with the quarrel with the brave Biscayan" (II. 3).

In many of the titles of his chapters, Cervantes anticipates the reality which Don Quixote is to misinterpret. For example, the title of chapter 8 does not speak of giants but of "the frightful and heretofore unimagined adventure of the windmills"; the title of chapter 16 speaks "of what happened to the ingenious knight in the inn which he imagined to be a castle"; the title of chapter

36 alludes to the battle which Don Quixote had "with some skins of red wine." If the reader examines all the titles, he will see that frequently the narrator discloses the nature of a given reality before his characters distort it.

Cervantes' tendency to explain everything can be represented with his oft-repeated phrase: "and such was the truth." How often he confirms facts with this phrase or some variant of it! When Sancho recognizes that the armies of chapter 18 are flocks of ewes and rams, the author confirms it on the spot: "And such was the truth, because the two flocks were already drawing near" (I. 18). Toward the end of Part II, Sancho says to his master: "And get up now your Grace to receive Don Gregorio; for it sounds to me as if everyone's excited, and he must be in the house by now." Then the author: "And such was the truth" (II. 65). Between these two examples many more may be found.[5] The narrator is the arbiter of the difficulties offered by reality. His refrain "and such was the truth" confirms it. If it were Cervantes' intention that the reader consider reality problematical, would he not have to conceal a bit his own confident attitude toward it? For him, as for the reader, the truth of what happens in *Don Quixote* "floats above falsehood like oil upon water" (II. 10).

On writing this some years ago, I realized that the real—or apparent—confidence of the narrator in the presence of reality was a technical requirement of his novel. If he did not disclose the true nature of the realities that his characters were to misinterpret, how could we laugh at their misinterpretations? If there are no certain realities, there can be no discernible errors. I still believe this to be the truth, but not

5. Besides the phrase "and such was the truth," there are many others of similar intent: "and thus it was," "as was later learned," "as in fact it was," "the plan which Sansón had . . . was to do what the story tells later on."

the whole truth, because it ignores linguistic subtleties which I failed to notice when I wrote the article. At the end of this chapter we will concern ourselves once more with reality as seen by the narrator. For now, it may be advantageous to examine it in relation to the characters.

An illuminating way to approach reality is through the language in which it is expressed. To draw attention to the expressions we are to study, I shall put them in italics. Of all the words that may shed some light on our theme, the most conspicuous is *parecer*,[6] which means "to seem" or "to appear," and which will always be translated in one of these two ways. It is used hundreds of times and by everybody. In the short first chapter the author uses it seven times. Here are the instances. Of the impression which certain books of chivalry made on Don Quixote we read: "none *seemed* as good as those which Feliciano de Silva composed, because the clarity of his prose and those complicated passages *seemed* to him as precious as pearls"; of his decision to become a knight-errant: "it *seemed* to him both proper and necessary"; of his reconstructed headpiece: "the ease with which he had smashed it to bits did not fail to *seem* bad to him"; of his nag: "finally he came to call him Rocinante, a name which *seemed* to him noble, sonorous and significant"; of Aldonza Lorenzo: "it *seemed* to him right to give to her the title of lady of his thoughts"; of Dulcinea del Toboso: "a name which *seemed* to him musical and rare and significant." There are instances in which *seem* figures five times on a single page: for example, when the Priest and his friends for the first time see Dorotea dis-

6. Writing in 1947, William Fichter pointed out the frequency and importance of *parecer* in Cervantes' vocabulary, but without indicating that a serious study of its use existed. See his "Estudios cervantinos recientes," *NRFH*, 2 (1948), 99-100. It is true that Américo Castro has *parecer* very much in mind when he writes on *Don Quixote*. Besides what he says in chapter 2 of *El pensamiento de Cervantes*, see pp. 431-434 of his *España en su historia* (Buenos Aires, 1948); and his recent Prólogo to *El ingenioso hidalgo Don Quijote de la Mancha* (Mexico, 1963).

guised as a peasant youth (I. 28), or when the dispute over Mambrino's helmet and the packsaddle begins (I. 45). One cannot doubt the extraordinary frequency with which *seem* is found throughout the book. This in itself is important. Its constant echo in the ear of the reader can not help but influence the impression he receives of the quixotic world.

The examples of *seem* already cited belong to the indirect discourse of modern novels. By means of this device, we penetrate into the inner life of the characters and learn about their opinions, their impressions, the face that the world wears for them. The author achieves the same end by putting *seem* directly into the mouths of his characters, and these are the two principal uses of the word. To examine them systematically, paying special attention to what the characters express with *seem*, we may begin with Don Quixote.

Before receiving the muleteers' fierce stoning, Don Quixote commends himself to Dulcinea: "With this, it *seemed* to him, he gained so much courage, that if all the muleteers in the world attacked him, he wouldn't retreat a step" (I. 3). A little after leaving the first inn, we read that the knight "had not gone far, when from a thicket of a woods, which was there on his right, it *seemed* to him some faint words came forth" (I. 4). At the end of the adventure with Andrés: "And in this way was that wrong redressed by the valorous Don Quixote, who was very pleased with the result, for it *seemed* to him that he had made a most happy and high beginning to his knight-errantry" (I. 4). Don Quixote sees a troop of some thirteen men on the road: "No sooner had Don Quixote made them out when he imagined this to be a matter for new adventure; and by imitating as near as it *seemed* possible to him the encounters he had read in his books, it *seemed* to him that here came a made-to-order one which he intended to undertake" (I. 4). On entering the Sierra Morena: "As soon as Don Quixote entered those mountains, his heart was gladdened, those places *seeming* to him well suited for the adventures he sought" (I. 23). On seeing the fury of the indignant squadron from the braying village, Don Quixote "took off in a cloud of dust, and without thinking of Sancho nor of the danger in which he was leaving him, he got as far away as it *seemed* necessary for him to feel safe" (II. 28). These are sufficient examples to give an idea of this use of *seem*, which serves to reveal to us the impressions, opinions, or judgments that the changing circumstances of his life provoke in the hero. This use of *seem* does not represent a semantic novelty, but the insistence with which Cervantes uses it is worth noting. It would have been possible to suppress it in most of the examples, saying, for instance: "with this he gained so much courage . . ."; "he hadn't gone far when he heard . . ."; "by imitating as near as possible the encounters he had read about in his books . . ."; "he got far enough away to feel safe." It would have been possible, but Cervantes preferred to express the reactions of his hero toward the world in a way that makes no firm commitment to reality.

More interesting than the examples of *seem* applied by the narrator to Don Quixote are those placed directly in his mouth. Many of them only express simple judgments or opinions: "it seems to me," "seemingly," "as it seems," etc. But there are also many which have to do with the deceptive appearances of a world at last so wearisome to the spirit of Don Quixote.

Don Quixote realizes very soon that not everyone sees things just as he does. Sancho, for example, sees windmills where he sees giants. Sancho insists they are windmills while recognizing some likeness to giants: "what in them *seem* to be arms are the vanes" (I. 8). In this adventure Don Quixote does not speak explicitly of appearances. Before attacking the giants, he attributes Sancho's mistaken vision to his fear. After the adventure is over, he blames his defeat on the intervention of the wizard Freston. When, in the adventure of the flocks, the squire hears the bleating of sheep instead of the noise of drums, the knight turns once again to the former's fear.[7] This time he does speak explicitly of appearances: "The fear that you have," said Don Quixote, "makes you, Sancho, so that you neither see nor hear right, because one of the effects of fear is to disturb the senses and make things not *appear* what they are" (I. 18). Here he confesses that to a specific individual, things can fail to appear what they are, but as he undertakes the adventure, he continues to believe that the root of error is in the individual and not in reality. After his defeat he resorts again to the explanation of enchantment, which seems to him a trick used by his enemy to deprive him of the glory he had hoped to achieve through victory in battle (I. 18). And one notices that it seems to him a trick of ephemeral effects, because he tells Sancho that if he follows the flocks of sheep, he will see how soon they change back to their original form.

A little later Don Quixote comes to understand that the effects of what he calls enchantment can be long-lasting and affect more persons than Sancho and himself. This lesson he owes above all to the basin-helmet: "Is it possible that as long as you've been traveling with me you haven't noticed that all matters of knights-errant *appear* to be chimeras, stupidities, and follies, and as though made wrong side first? And not because that's the way it is, but because always there wanders amongst us a throng of enchanters who change and alter all our things, and twist them according to their taste and according to their desire to favor or destroy us; and so, what to you *seems* a barber's basin *seems* to me Mambrino's helmet, and to another will *seem*

7. In the adventure of the lions Don Quixote again explains by fear the (to him) eccentric vision of Sancho.

something else" (I. 25). From what Don Quixote says right after these words, we know that he continues to regard himself as the one who sees things straight, but as time goes on, he comes to realize that he too can be fooled by the appearances of things:

> So, to set myself now to giving my opinion on a matter of so much confusion would be to fall into a rash judgment. As for what they say about this being a basin and not a helmet, I have already answered; but as to declaring whether that is a packsaddle or a harness, I don't dare make a definite decision; I shall let it depend exclusively on how it *seems* to your worships. Perhaps since you have not been knighted as I have, the enchantments of this place will not affect you, and your understandings will be free, and you will be able to judge the things of this castle as they really and truly are, and not as they *appear* to me [I. 45].

Here it is fitting to remember again the words pronounced by Don Quixote at the end of the adventure of "The Parliament of Death": "and now I say that it's necessary to touch appearances with one's hand to avoid being deceived" (II. 11). Don Quixote will insist that things are as he wishes them to be ("although they *seem* to be water mills, they are not," II. 29), but he will no longer doubt how difficult it is to distinguish them properly.

What has been said about things can be extended to persons. They too present deceptive appearances, and the knight recognizes this as well. Here are some of the words he pronounced after dinner at the inn, where so many important knights and ladies were gathered: "Which of those living in this world that might enter now through the door of this castle and see us as we are would judge and believe that we are who we are?" (I. 37). When Sancho tries to persuade his master that his enchanters are the Priest and the Barber, Don Quixote readily admits not that they are but that they may bear that appearance: "it may well be that they *appear* to be the same ones, but don't you believe for a moment that they really and truly are. What you should believe and understand is that if they *seem* like them, as you say, it must be because those who have enchanted me have taken on that appearance and similarity" (I. 48). According to Don Quixote, this change of appearances is the work of enchanters, as is also the resemblance of Don Quixote to one of the knights conquered by the Knight of the Mirrors. The likeness throws Don Quixote into some confusion: "On the other hand, I see with my eyes and touch with my hands the impossibility of it being the same person" (II. 14). But he ends up conquering the Knight of the Mirrors and resolving his doubts with the well-known explanation: "You must also confess and believe . . . that the knight you conquered was not and could not have been Don Quixote of the Mancha, but another who *seemed* like him, as I confess and believe, that you, although you *seem* to be the Bachelor Sansón Carrasco, are not he, but someone who *seems* like him, and whom my enemies have placed before me in the likeness of his person" (II. 14).

Enchantment is not, however, the only thing that makes a person appear what he is not. Don Quixote rightfully supposes that Don Diego de Miranda takes him for a foolish and crazy man. To justify himself before Don Diego, he delivers a speech dotted with examples of *seem*. The burden of his speech is that his conduct seems mad only to those unacquainted with the code that governs it. He does not do foolish things but only what his code and destiny oblige him to do: "I, since it has been my lot to be of the number of knights-errant, cannot fail to undertake everything which *seems* to me to fall under the jurisdiction of my exercises" (II. 17).

Don Quixote recognizes that there are still other reasons

why people seem to be what they are not, and that it is very difficult to distinguish between the essence and the appearance of a person: "Nor are all who call themselves knights really knights through and through; because some are of gold, others of alloy, and all *appear* to be knights; but not all can stand the test of the touchstone of truth. There are low-born men who try to *appear* to be knights, and there are high-born knights who *seem* determined to *appear* to be low-born: The former raise themselves either by ambition or virtue; the latter lower themselves either by weakness or vice; and one must avail oneself of discreet knowledge to distinguish between these two kinds of knights, so *like-seeming* in name and so unlike in actions" (II. 6). Let it not escape us that it is the mad knight who declares that one must avail oneself of discreet knowledge in order really to know people.[8]

Don Quixote uses *seem* a great deal more than we have indicated in the quotations already recorded, but they will suffice to make manifest one of the ways Don Quixote expresses the complications of his world. The original source of his confusions is the literature he has read. The narrator has already told us this early in his book: "and as everything he thought, saw or imagined *seemed* to our adventurer to be made and behave in the style of what he had read . . ." (I. 2). But this is only a partial explanation. What has been presented up till now tends to demonstrate that reality can offer difficulties not easily explained. Studying *seem* as used by the other characters will shed more light on the subject.

Like his master, Sancho makes use of *seem* to emit simple

8. The frequency with which *discreto* (discreet) and its derivatives figure in Cervantes' writings has already been noticed. See Margaret J. Bates, *"Discreción" in the Works of Cervantes: A Semantic Study* (Washington, 1945). Perhaps it is mentioned so much in *Don Quixote* because one needs a great deal of discretion to make one's way among the misleading appearances of the quixotic world.

judgments or opinions not worth our examining here. As we saw a short while ago, Sancho uses *seem* for admitting similarities tending to confuse: *vanes-arms* (I. 8). He also uses it—or a synonym—mischievously. For example, when speaking of the basin-helmet: "I'm laughing . . . to think what a big head that pagan who owned this helmet had, which *seems* like nothing so much as a true barber's basin" (I. 21); or when speaking of the barber's ass: "tell me, your worship, what shall we do with this dapple-gray horse which *seems* like a gray ass" (I. 21); or when enchanting Dulcinea: "And is it possible that three hackneys, or whatever their names are, white as the driven snow, *seem* like little donkeys to your worship?" (II. 10).[9]

Sancho typically uses *seem* to give an impressionistic explanation of phenomena that he does not understand well. For example, after the first hubbub in the inn, he says to his master: "it *seems* only that all the devils have been at me tonight" (I. 17); or on resisting the washing of his beard: "for such *cirimonies* and soapings as these *seem* more like jokes than kind hospitality" (II. 32). Like his master, the servant also sees a connection between extraordinary appearances and enchantment: "for since everything that's happened to him is by enchantment, perhaps what to us *seems* like an hour, must *seem* there [Cave of Montesinos] like three days and nights" (II. 23). Sometimes Sancho's reactions anticipate events, as when he speaks of the Holy Brotherhood after the adventure of the galley slaves: "it *seems* to me that their arrows are already buzzing about my ears" (I. 23). Other times his reactions are retrospective, as when he arrived alone at the inn where he had been tossed in a blanket: "and he had scarcely seen it when it *seemed* to him that he was flying through the air again" (I. 26).

Appearances give Sancho a great deal to think about, especially the appearances of people. On seeing the Knight

9. Other examples may be found in I. 25 and II. 31, 41.

of the Mirrors unhorsed and looking like Sansón Carrasco, Sancho says, "It *seems* to me, my lord, that, just in case, your worship should thrust and drive the sword into the mouth of this man who *seems* like the bachelor Sansón Carrasco: perhaps you will kill in him one of your enchanter enemies" (II. 14). His wanting to kill the person who looks like Sansón Carrasco reveals to what extent Sancho too can mistrust appearances. His mistrust arises out of the discrepancy he discovers between the Bachelor's conduct and what Sancho believes he knows about him. Nevertheless, he soon begins to wonder whether those who look like Sansón Carrasco and Tomé Cecial may not really be Sansón Carrasco and Tomé Cecial: "Well, sir, what shall we say," replied Sancho, "about this business of that knight, whoever he may be, *seeming* like the bachelor Carrasco, and his squire, like my old friend Tomé Cecial? And if that is enchantment, as your worship has said, weren't there any other two in the world that might *seem* like one another?" (II. 16). In the episode of the pretended disenchantment of Dulcinea, Sancho has to admit that her appearance is not in accord with what he thought she was like: "let the world enjoy the beauty of the lady Doña Dulcinea del Toboso, since, as it *appears* and contrary to what I thought, she really is beautiful" (II. 35). After the adventure of Clavileño, he sees and hears the Duke's majordomo speak, and believes he notices a resemblance to the Countess Trifaldi. Among other words, he uses these to his master: "it *seemed* like nothing so much as the voice of the Trifaldi woman sounding in my ears. All right now: I'll be quiet; but I won't fail to keep my eyes open from now on to see whether she reveals any other sign to confirm or destroy my suspicion" (II. 44). But no matter how wide open Sancho keeps his eyes, he will continue to meet situations that he can not fathom. The culminating example comes with the defeat of Don Quixote at the hands of the Knight of the

White Moon. On this ill-starred occasion Cervantes presents Sancho as follows: "Sancho, all grief-stricken and sad, did not know what to say or do: it *seemed* to him that that whole affair was taking place in a dream and was a matter of enchantment" (II. 64).

The other characters in the novel do not speak the word *seem* so often as the knight and his squire; still and all, they speak it often enough. Like Don Quixote and Sancho, they use it to express simple judgments and opinions of this type: "the title of the novel doesn't *seem* to me bad" (I. 32). Occasionally, the word is repeated as though to be sure that it does not escape the reader's attention: "the way it *seemed* to him *seemed* all right to her" (I. 34).

Apart from this simple and very frequent use, perhaps it is employed most to speak of appearances. The innkeeper's wife, on seeing Don Quixote so black and blue, "said that that *appeared* more like blows than a fall" (I. 16). To the innkeeper's wife, her daughter, and Maritornes, Don Quixote "*appeared* . . . a different kind of man from those they were used to" (I. 16). Luscinda says to a man on the street, "Brother, if you are a Christian as you *appear* to be . . ." (I. 27). So much talk of the appearances of reality presents the characters as though they were forewarned against it: Vivaldo, for example, speaks not of what Don Quixote is like but of what he appears to be like: "She [Dulcinea] would consider herself fortunate to have the whole world know that she is loved and served by such a knight as your worship *appears* to be" (I. 13). The Captive speaks in a similar manner to Luscinda and the other ladies of the inn: "I value highly . . . the favor offered, which, on such an occasion and from such people as you *appear* to be, is clearly very great" (I. 17). These appearances are presented at times to justify opinions or actions. When she hears Sancho speak of kingdoms, the innkeeper's wife says, "Well, how does it happen . . . you don't have, to judge by *appearances,* so much as an earldom?" (I. 16). After hearing Sancho speak of his celestial vision, the Duchess says, "Friend Sancho, mind what you're saying: because, as it *seems,* you didn't see the earth" (II. 41). Of the coral necklace Teresa says, "Let me wear it a few days around my neck, for it truly *appears* to gladden my heart" (II. 50).

On one occasion Zoraida recognizes that one and the same action can present two faces to two people: "even if I wanted not to go with them and to remain at home, it would have been impossible for me, so fast did my soul hurry me toward this work which to me *appears* to be as good as you, beloved father, judge it to be bad" (I. 41). Cardenio recognizes that things are not always what they seem; Doña Rodríguez is of the same opinion. In gossipy confidence she speaks to Don Quixote of the Duchess' appearance of health: "That complexion, which *seems* as smooth as a burnished sword . . . and that graceful air with which she treads the ground so haughtily that it *appears* as though she were showering health wherever she goes" (II. 48). Dorotea has learned that falsehood can appear to be truth: "he began to speak to me such words that I don't know how it is possible for deceit to have the skill to make them *seem* true" (I. 28).

There are cases in which the characters move in a veritable labyrinth of *seemings* and *appearings.* A good example is that of the dispute over the helmet and the packsaddle. We have already quoted something of what Don Quixote said on that occasion. His last words to the assembled group were: "and you may be able to judge of the things of this castle as they really and truly are, and not as they *seemed* to me" (I. 45). At this point Cervantes says, "For those who were informed of Don Quixote's humor, all this was a matter of much laughter; but for those who knew nothing about it, it *seemed* the greatest nonsense in the world, especially to the four servants of Don Luis, to Don

Luis himself, and to three other travelers who by chance
had arrived at the inn and who *seemed* to be officers of the
Holy Brotherhood, which in truth they were" (I. 45).
Then, Fernando says he is "tired of taking so many *opinions*
[*pareceres*] and that it is nonsense to say that this is a
packsaddle rather than the trappings of a horse" (I. 45).
Then the traveling barber says that they are mistaken and
"may my soul appear before God as surely as it *appears* to
me to be a packsaddle and not the trappings of a horse" (I.
45). Next, one of Don Luis' servants: "Unless this is some
kind of deliberate joke, I cannot persuade myself that men
of such good understanding as are or *appear* to be all those
here present should dare to say and affirm that this is not a
basin nor that a packsaddle; but as I see that they do affirm
and say it, I conclude that there is some mystery in main-
taining something so contrary to what truth and experience
itself reveal" (I. 45). Almost at once a violent quarrel
breaks out. When peace is restored, the narrator concludes:
"In this way was that storm of violence pacified by authority of Agramante and the prudence of King Sobrino;
but the enemy of concord and the rival of peace, seeing
himself despised and mocked and seeing how little fruit
he had gathered from having involved everybody in so
confused a *labyrinth*, decided to try his hand again at
stirring up new quarrels and anxieties" (I. 45). On the
previous page the narrator has described the situation as
consisting of a "chaos, multitude, and *labyrinth* of things."

We have recorded many examples of *seem*, and many
more could be cited. But perhaps the examples already exhibited justify the following conclusion: The persons who
inhabit Don Quixote's world have to deal with that world
largely on the basis of impressions and appearances. Often
these impressions and appearances do not lead them to an
adequate interpretation of reality. This we have already
seen, but it is important to consider it now in the light of

other linguistic evidence abundantly scattered throughout the novel.

One of the constant preoccupations of the characters is to interpret the world about them. There is no linguistic evidence that testifies more copiously to this preoccupation than what we may call "conjectural language." It is accurate to say that this kind of language is even more abundant than the language of appearances. The phrase most often used by Cervantes to express conjecture is *deber de*, and it occurs more frequently than *parecer*. It means "must," as in the sentence: "He must be around here somewhere." It is important to the thesis of this chapter to demonstrate the extraordinary frequency with which this *must* is used by Cervantes. To impose some order on the many examples to be quoted, I shall examine conjectural language in relation both to what it tries to discover and to the evidence on which it rests.

There is frequent conjecture about the presumed actions of various people. Thus, for example, the Priest says it is necessary to burn Don Quixote's books "so that they won't give occasion to whomever reads them to do what my good friend *must* have done" (I. 5). He says these words before he has any way of knowing for sure what Don Quixote has done on his first sally. On the night of his visit to El Toboso, Sancho excuses himself for not being able to find Dulcinea's house, saying to his master that the latter "*must* have seen it thousands of times" (II. 9). Sanchica, on seeing the letter and the coral necklace brought by the page of the Duke and Duchess, conjectures that Don Quixote "*must* have given father the government or earldom that he had repeatedly promised him" (II. 50). Claudia Jerónima, on reporting her violent encounter with Don Vicente, says, "I shot at him with this shotgun and also with these two pistols, and, I believe, I *must* have buried more than two bullets in his body" (II. 60).

There is conjecture also about what people are like. On seeing the large and incomplete helmet of Mambrino, Don Quixote imagines that its former owner "*must* have had an uncommonly large head" (I. 21). On hearing Sancho's laudatory description of his daughter, Tomé Cecial exclaims: "what a strong lass the little rogue *must* be" (II. 13).

Don Quixote's apparently absurd words and conduct motivate many conjectures. His description of the basin-helmet causes Sancho to say, "Because anyone hearing your worship say that a barber's basin is Mambrino's helmet . . . what is he to think but that he who says and affirms such things *must* be addle-brained" (I. 25). Here is a goatherd's reaction to Don Quixote: "as near as I can make out, either your worship is joking, or this gentleman *must* be empty in the head" (I. 52). Concerning the reaction of the Gentleman in Green: "From these last words of Don Quixote, the traveler guessed that Don Quixote *must* be some simpleton, and he waited for other words to confirm it" (II. 16). On reproaching the Duke, his chaplain says of Don Quixote: "I imagine that he *must* not be so much a simpleton as Your Excellency pretends" (II. 31). Later, Tosilos offers this opinion: "Without doubt, friend Sancho, your master *must* be a madman" (II. 66).

There is recourse to conjecture—as well as to enchantment—to explain mysterious happenings or phenomena. The hubbub in the former loft of the inn awoke the innkeeper, who "at once imagined that it *must* be Maritornes' quarrels" (I. 16). As we recalled earlier, Don Quixote attributes to enchanters his being carried off in an oxcart, but since on this occasion enchantment does not completely satisfy him as an explanation of what is occurring, he exclaims, "By God, it fills me with confusion! But perhaps the chivalry and enchantment of our times *must* follow a different road than they used to" (I. 47). The depressing outcome of the adventure of the enchanted boat pushes Don Quixote to another extreme explanation: "In this, two valiant enchanters *must* have clashed, the one frustrating what the other attempts" (II. 29). Don Vicente conjectures that his bad fortune explains the violent procedure of Claudia Jerónima: "my bad fortune *must* have carried you this news, so that in jealousy you would take my life" (II. 60).

There are conversations and accounts overflowing with *must's*. In them it is not rare for a single person to use it two or more times in succession. Dorotea, on speaking of Don Fernando's lascivious appetite, says, "All this reserve on my part, which he *must* have taken for disdain, *must* have further whetted his lascivious appetite, because this is the name I wish to give to the love he showed me" (I. 28). When Don Quixote asks the Bachelor if there are other things to correct in his story, the latter answers, "Yes, there *must* be . . . but none *must* be of the importance of those already mentioned" (II. 4). Perhaps it is unnecessary to say that nobody uses *must* so often as Sancho and Don Quixote. When the former finds out that Aldonza Lorenzo is Dulcinea, he is prodigal in his use of it: "And I'd like to be on my way just to see her; because I haven't seen her for many days and she *must* be much changed. . . . And I confess to your worship, Señor Don Quixote, that until now I have been misled in one respect; I really and truly thought that my lady Dulcinea *must* be some princess with whom your worship was in love, or some other person deserving of the rich presents which your worship has sent her, both the Biscayan and the galley slaves, and the many others that there *must* be, as the victories *must* have been many which your grace has won" (I. 25). Don Quixote too is prodigal in the use of *must*. On learning of the issues in the Duchess' legs he exclaims, "I wouldn't have believed it if barefoot friars had told me so; but since my lady Doña Rodríguez says so, it *must* be true. But such issues and in such places *must* not exude humors but liquid amber gris.

71

Truly I am now convinced that this business of issues *must* be important to health" (II. 48).

Conjecture finds support in everything: intuition, previous knowledge, intimate needs and desires, and, above all, appearances. This is manifest in many examples. In some of those quoted below, appearances and conjectures are expressed by the now-familiar words *seem* and *must*. In the scrutiny of Don Quixote's library the Priest conjectures, because of their small size, what certain still unexamined books are: "These . . . *must* not be books of chivalry but of poetry" (I. 6). Before the battle with the Biscayan, Don Quixote says, "Those dark shapes that *appear*[10] there *must* be, and without a doubt are, some enchanters who have kidnapped a princess" (I. 8). When the knight calls one cloud of dust an army, the squire replies, "By that token there *must* be two . . . because from the opposite direction another similar cloud is rising" (I. 18). On the brink of the adventure "that without artifice truly *seemed* to be one," Don Quixote exclaimed: "this, without doubt, Sancho, *must* be a great and dangerous adventure" (I. 19). When the veiled and sad Luscinda arrived with her escort at the inn, the Priest asked a servant who she was, and he replied, "as far as one can gather from her dress, she is a nun, or is going to be one, which is more likely, and perhaps because it *must* not be her will to take the veil, she is sad, as she *appears*" (I. 36).

The characters of *Don Quixote* spend their lives conjecturing about the appearances of the world, and they indicate the explicit basis of their conjectures with notable frequency. A good example of this is the finding in Sierra Morena of the rotten suitcase and cushion. After examining

10. Here *parecen* means *aparecen*—that is to say, "appear" in the primary sense of "come into sight." Consequently, this example and perhaps a few more do not signify exactly what most of our examples do, but it doesn't matter. All represent something typical of Cervantes' way of presenting things: first what is seen, then its interpretation.

them, Don Quixote says, "It *seems* to me, Sancho, and nothing else is possible, that some stray traveler *must* have passed through this sierra and been attacked by thieves, who *must* have killed him." Shortly thereafter, the knight reads a sonnet found in the suitcase, and Sancho says, "By this poem . . . one can learn nothing, unless it be a clue to solve the mystery." Then Don Quixote: "Upon my faith he *must* be a reasonably good poet, or I know little of the art" (I. 23). Finally, the narrator characterizes Don Quixote's mental state as follows: "The Knight of the Sad Countenance remained with a strong desire to know who the owner of the suitcase might be, *conjecturing* from the sonnet and the letter, from the gold coins and from the fine shirts, that he *must* be a high-born lover whom his lady's disdain and ill-treatment *must* have led to some desperate end" (I. 23). In another episode the Priest says to the young farmer, who turns out to be Dorotea in disguise: "What your clothes, my lady, deny us, your hair reveals: clear *indications* that the causes which have disguised your beauty *must* not be of small moment" (I. 28).

All the characters live attentive to the signs that may orient them in their dealings with the world. The Christian horseman who receives the captive on the beach of Velez Málaga says, "by the *signs* and *samples* of your clothes and those of this whole company, I understand that you have had a miraculous liberation" (I. 41). The narrator tells us that Housekeeper and Niece "by a *thousand signs* were *inferring* that their uncle and master wanted to break away a third time" (II. 6). Later Sancho says, "By a *thousand signs*, I have seen that this master of mine is mad enough to be put in a strait jacket" (II. 10). Everybody catches at whatever straws of evidence will help him interpret the circumstances in which he lives. For example, Sancho and his master were dozing in a wood when the latter heard a noise and woke his squire. Among other things, the knight said, "But listen, for, as it *seems to me,* he is tuning a lute or a guitar, and *by the way* he is spitting and clearing his throat, he *must* be getting ready to sing something." And Sancho answers, "Upon my faith so he is . . . and he *must* be a lovelorn knight." Then Don Quixote: "There are no knight-errants not in love . . . and let us listen to him, because *by the thread of* his song we will reach the center of his thoughts" (II. 12). Don Quixote even theorizes about the possibility of solving inner mysteries following external clues. For example, in these words addressed to Sancho before sending him to El Toboso to speak to Dulcinea: "finally, my son, watch all her actions and movements; because if you recount them to me as they occurred, I will be able to *infer* what she keeps hidden in her innermost heart regarding my love for her; for you must know, Sancho, if you don't know it already, that between lovers the external actions and movements which they reveal, when dealing with their love affair, are true messengers bearing news of what takes place in the depths of their souls" (II. 10).

The linguistic devices already exhibited by no means exhaust the possibilities available in Spanish to express conjecture or probability. The future and conditional tenses also serve this purpose, and Cervantes used them copiously. Since these uses are not natural to English, I will record the Spanish verb in parentheses to document the attitude my examples were chosen to illustrate. To the "Muñatón" referred to by his niece, Don Quixote answers, "He probably said *(diría)* Freston" (I. 7). The future may be combined with *seem:* "What can this be *(será),* Sancho; it *seems* that my skull is turning soft, or my brains are dissolving, or that I am sweating from head to foot" (II. 17). Sometimes the future is combined with *deber de:* "What's probable *(será),* when you come right down to it, is that some company of actors *must* be within" (I. 43). To record here still more examples of the future of probability would add nothing new to what we have already discovered in the other devices, of which I have cited only a small fraction. In support of this claim, perhaps it will suffice to say that in Part II alone, conjecture is expressed more than 170 times by means of the verb *deber de*.

We have seen to the point of boredom that the characters in *Don Quixote* spend their lives guessing, inferring, conjecturing, trying to orient themselves by all kinds of signs and clues. That is to say, we have seen how much it matters to them and how difficult it is for them to interpret correctly the realities amid which they live. At the beginning of this chapter we saw that Cervantes tended to define these realities for his readers, and we suggested that to do so was a technical requirement of his novel. But we also suggested that his presentation of reality might hold subtleties in need of still further investigation. Does Cervantes establish fully and beyond all doubt the precise nature of the realities he presents, or does he allow them some shadowy margin of ambiguity? An answer to this question may be found in the same linguistic resources that served to reveal the characters' intercourse with reality.

Having considered the word *seem* as applied to or spoken by the characters, it is necessary to see how the narrator uses it in his own name. He employs it most often to present the appearance of persons, animals, and things. Of Rocinante, for example, we may read that "so willingly did he set out that he *appeared* not to touch the ground with his feet" (I. 4); or, "it *appeared* at that instant that he had sprouted wings" (I. 19); or, "he was of flesh, although he *appeared* to be of wood" (I. 43). When Vivaldo was about to read another of the dead Grisóstomo's papers, "he was interrupted by a marvelous vision—or so it *appeared*—that unexpectedly offered itself to view" (I. 14). As Dorotea finishes her story, Cervantes says, "She who *appeared* to be such a beautiful woman said all this without stopping" (I.

28). On hearing Cardenio's voice, "Luscinda behaved so that she *appeared* to be out of her mind" (I. 36). The verb *to show (mostrar,* which for the sake of more natural English, we shall sometimes translate by *look like),* also serves the narrator to present appearances. For example, that of the Captive: "in his dress he looked like a Christian recently arrived from the land of the Moors . . . he *showed* in gentle bearing that had he been well dressed, they would have taken him for a person of quality and good breeding. . . . On entering, he asked for a room, and since he was told there was none available in the inn, he *showed* a sad countenance" (I. 37). Home again after his second sally, "Don Quixote *seemed* like nothing so much as mummy flesh" (II. 25). In the inn the guests saw Master Peter's monkey "speaking, or so it *appeared,* in his ear" (II. 25). Of the cats in Don Quixote's room: "it *appeared* that a legion of devils were scrambling about in it" (II. 46). About Governor Sancho Panza's first supper we read: "A personage who later *showed* himself to be a doctor stationed himself at the Governor's side . . . one who *appeared* to be a student said grace" (II. 47). Don Quixote and Sancho came across some men carrying images for an altarpiece: "the first image, which *showed* itself to be that of Saint George on horseback . . . The whole image *appeared* like a golden ember" (II. 58). These examples represent the pronounced tendency in Cervantes' writing of putting before his characters not what things are but rather what they appear to be. Perhaps the most surprising aspect of this tendency is that which reveals Cervantes renouncing a novelist's omniscience. A few examples will make the point.

In order to keep vigil over his arms, Don Quixote placed them across the watering trough in the corral of the inn. A muleteer came along and removed them: "Seeing which, Don Quixote lifted his eyes to heaven, and turning his thoughts—as it *appeared*—to his lady . . ." (I. 3). If the narrator doesn't know whether or not his hero turned his thoughts to his lady, who does? To explain the impulse that came upon Sancho to do what no one else could do for him, the narrator says, "At this point, it *appears* that either the cold of the morning or something laxative that Sancho might have eaten or some natural urge . . ." (I. 20). He ventures an opinion about Lothario's conduct: "and it *appears* that all of Lothario's good sense failed him at this point" (I. 34). In the middle of the conversation between the two squires, the author says, "Sancho often spat, or so it *seemed*, a kind of sticky saliva" (II. 13). Don Quixote had traveled but a short distance from the house of Don Diego, "when he met two 'sort of like' clerics or students . . .[11] One of the students was carrying, as though in a portmanteau, what *seemed* like a piece of fine scarlet cloth" (II. 19). During the festivities associated with Camacho's wedding, there arrived "a man dressed in what *seemed* like a black tunic trimmed with flamelike crimson patches" (II. 21). Shortly after the adventure of Montesinos' Cave, Don Quixote and Sancho bumped into a youth described by the narrator as follows: "He carried a sword over his shoulder, to which was attached, to judge by appearances, a bundle of clothes, which apparently *must* have been his breeches or pantaloons . . . he was *probably* eighteen or nineteen years old, gay of face, and *apparently* agile of body" (II. 24). In the nocturnal darkness of Don Quixote's bedroom they spanked Doña Rodríguez with "what *seemed* like a slipper" (II. 48). After the episode of the bulls Don Quixote and Sancho hurried "to reach an inn which *seemed* to be dimly visible about a league off" (II. 59). On reaching the inn, the

11. To say "two 'sort of like' clerics or students" (*dos como clérigos o estudiantes*) represents another linguistic device tending to show how difficult it is to capture reality in words. It crops up with considerable frequency in the language of both the characters and the narrator. The latter will say, for example, "necessity or stupidity" (I. 33); "grove or woods" (II. 9); "woods, live-oak grove, or forest" (II. 10); "castle or house" (II. 19); "pleasure house or castle" (II. 31).

two retire to their room. At this point the author remarks, "It *seems* that in another room next to theirs . . . Don Quixote heard someone say . . ." (II. 59). From this other room there came forth two gentlemen, or so they *seemed* . . ." (II. 59). How did Don Quixote and Sancho discover the dead bodies of the bandits hung in the woods near Barcelona? According to Cervantes, "*seemingly* they raised their eyes . . ." (II. 60). How did it happen that the Knight of the White Moon failed to kill Don Quixote in their dangerous encounter? Simply because at the critical moment "he raised his lance, *seemingly* on purpose . . ." (II. 64). I have cited all these examples to be sure no one can legitimately doubt that the tendency in question is truly representative of Cervantes' style. Is it not curious that he chooses not to know with certainty so many details of the world he himself has created? [12]

One of the things that Cervantes prefers not to know precisely is the age of his characters. On the first page of the novel we learn that Don Quixote was going on fifty, that his housekeeper was over forty, and that his niece was not yet twenty. Often these approximations are presented as the apparent ages of the characters in question. Of the dead Grisóstomo, we read that he was "*apparently* thirty years old" (I. 13). Doña Clara was "*apparently* sixteen or less" (I. 42); the Knight of the Green Coat "*showed* his age to be fifty" (II. 35); the maiden who played the part of Dulcinea was said to be "*apparently* between sixteen and twenty" (II. 35); the lass discovered during Governor Sancho's nocturnal patrol revealed "the face of a woman *apparently* sixteen or more" (II. 49). Sanchica "*appeared* to be more or less fourteen years old" (II. 50); her mother "*looked* as if she was over forty" (II. 49); Roque Guinart "*showed* his age to be thirty-four" (II. 60); Claudia Jeró-

12. Among the things he chooses not to name, the first is the village in La Mancha where Don Quixote lived.

nima was "*apparently* no more than twenty" (II. 60); the age of Ana Félix "*apparently* was less than twenty" (II. 63); Don Gregorio was "*apparently* from seventeen to eighteen years of age" (II. 65). These examples represent only those approximate ages explicitly related to appearances. With three or four exceptions, the ages of all the characters are presented as approximations, and this leads us to another important characteristic of Cervantes' narrative style: that of recording in approximative language many of the circumstances of his characters.

It is important to recognize how abundant the language of approximation is in Cervantes' linguistic arsenal. Perhaps this can be rapidly achieved by citing merely fragments of sentences. Cervantes' characters also express themselves in approximations, but the examples cited below all represent the novelist himself. Here is a small collection: "thirty or forty windmills" (I. 8); "up to six shepherds" (I. 13); "up to twenty shepherds" (I. 13); "who numbered more than twenty persons" (I. 17); "the dead sheep, which were more than seven" (I. 18); "they discovered up to twenty figures in white surplices" (I. 19); "up to twelve men were coming on foot" (I. 22); "the discovered crowns exceeded one hundred" (I. 23); "they had not walked a hundred steps" (I. 28); "up to two leagues from there" (I. 29); "three or four days from then" (II. 4); "the cooks were more than fifty in number" (II. 20); "up to twelve farmers" (II. 20); "up to twenty-four shepherds" (II. 20); "up to twelve duennas" (II. 38); "a village with up to a thousand inhabitants" (II. 45); "up to a dozen men" (II. 58); "more than forty live bandits" (II. 60); "with up to six servants" (II. 60); "up to fourteen or fifteen banks of oars" (II. 63); "there *must* have been up to thirty-six people" (II. 63); "up to ten men on horses and four or five on foot" (II. 68); "up to six duennas" (II. 69).

Cervantes tends to describe the attendant circumstances

of his narrative with the imprecision illustrated above. When he treats of these circumstances with meticulous precision, it is usually in a spirit of mockery. For example, he has La Dolorida say: "from here to the Kingdom of Candaya, if one travels by land, it is five thousand leagues, give or take two; but if one travels by air and in a straight line, it is three thousand two hundred and twenty-seven" (II. 40). This is the style of the romances of chivalry. Because of their value as a contrast to Cervantes' style, it may be worth while to recall here some words spoken by Don Quixote in defense of the truth of the romances of chivalry: "could they be lies, wearing such an appearance of truth, since they tell us about the father, the mother, the homeland, the relatives, the age, the town, and the deeds, point by point and day by day, that such a knight or knights did?" (I. 50).[13] This is exactly the way Cervantes does not tell his story, and letting his creatures move in a world not rigidly defined is one of the secrets of the autonomy they seem to enjoy.

We have seen that the narrator builds his story, as the characters do their lives, on the basis of impressions, appearances, and approximations. Like them, he too expresses himself by conjecture. Of the Manchegan gentleman's name he tells us: "By plausible conjecture one may understand that his name was Quejana" (I. i); "he *must* have been called Quijada, and not Quesada" (I. i); "Señor Quijana—so he *must* have been called when he was in his right mind" (I. 5). Of the Biscayan: "Don Sancho Azpeitia, such *must* have been his name" (I. 9). Of Sancho: "Sancho Zancas,

13. In his role as supposed translator of the novel, Cervantes explicitly rejects precise and detailed descriptions: "Here the author paints all the circumstances of Don Diego's house, painting for us in them all that is contained in the house of a rich country squire; but it seemed proper to the translator of this story to pass over in silence these and other similar trifling details, because they did not accord with the principal purpose of the story, whose strength rests on truth more than on dull digressions" (II. 18).

and it *must* have been that he had, as *shown* by the picture, a big belly, a short waist, and long shanks, and that's why they *must* have called him Panza and Zancas" (I. 9). The author conjectures about the Galician mares: "But they, as it *appeared*, *must* have felt more like grazing than anything else, and they received him with their hooves and their teeth" (I. 15). He conjectures about distances: "It *must* have been another hundred steps they walked" (I. 20); or "three quarters of a league they *must* have walked" (I. 29). He conjectures about the time of day: "it *must* have been two in the afternoon when they reached the village" (II. 17); or "it *must* have been four in the afternoon when the sun . . ." (II. 23). He conjectures about the hat of the traveling barber: "it began to rain, and so that his hat, which *must* have been new, would not get spotted . . ." (I. 20). He conjectures about Quiteria's looks: "The beautiful Quiteria was somewhat pale, and it *must* have been because of the bad night prospective brides always spend" (II. 21). He conjectures about the Duke's private chaplain: "the grave cleric who went out with the Duke and Duchess to receive Don Quixote *must* have been one of those . . ." (II. 31). He conjectures about the reason for Altisidora's moving: "At this point, Altisidora, who *must* have been tired from lying on her back so long, turned on her side" (II. 69).[14]

In my article quoted at the beginning of this chapter, I suggested that Cervantes' characters tended to misinterpret

14. It would be difficult to identify and enumerate all the subtle ways in which Cervantes presents a world of undefined or partially undefined realities. In addition to the linguistic resources already studied, one might mention two more: contradictory phrases like *discretas locuras* (discreet mad deeds or words [II. Prologue]) and the figure of speech called zeugma. This figure serves well to suggest the multiple possibilities of the world. Cervantes uses it on numerous occasions, but since it is tricky to translate, I will recall only one example. Dorotea refers to her seduction by saying: "When my maid again left the room, I ceased to be one" (I. 28).

reality because they saw it in the distorting mirror of their illusions, and it is certain that their illusions do influence their interpretations. We will go into this in detail in the following chapter. In this chapter our purpose is to concentrate on the role of reality itself. We have observed that Cervantes makes his characters live in a world favorable to illusion. Often he fails to provide them with sufficient data for the proper interpretation of the realities they have to confront, and he often presents these realities cloaked in ambiguities and appearances conducive to error. We have already cited the adventure "which, without any artifice at all, truly *seemed* to be one" (I. 19). What is the meaning of this "truly" used by the narrator to modify "seemed"? Clearly, it means that one would not have to be mad or deluded to interpret as a possible adventure the weird procession advancing along the road, because in truth it bore the semblance of adventure. Earlier we said that the narrator tended to establish the true nature of certain realities before his characters misinterpreted them. Now we can see that he often established appearances in such a way as to justify their misinterpretations. Here are a few more examples of the curious phrasing he sometimes used. Of Dorotea's exposed leg he says: "*without any doubt at all it seemed* of white alabaster" (I. 28). On describing the fake scene of Dulcinea's disenchantment, he writes: "To this veritable tempest, another was added to enlarge it, and it was that four battles *truly seemed* to be occurring at the same time" (II. 34). The Countess Trifaldi causes herself to be preceded by sad music that disturbs all who hear it; note the narrator's comment: "because *really* and *truly* the sound they heard was most sad and melancholy" (II. 36).

Cervantes establishes a fair number of firm realities to serve as a screen on which his characters may project their aberrations. Of this there can be little doubt; but some of his protestations that incline us to this conclusion permit another interpretation. If he so frequently sets himself up to be the arbiter of truth, may it not be in part because he wants the reader to notice how difficult it is to keep one's bearings amidst deceptive appearances and practical jokes? Isn't that what is suggested by phrases such as: "And the Duchess that day *really* and *truly* dispatched one of her pages" (II. 46)? Cervantes sometimes acts as though he too were on his guard against the deceptive realities of his own created world.[15]

We have listed many examples of *seem* and of *must*, perhaps too many. And one may say that some of them are trivial. But the frequency with which they occur is not trivial, nor does it fail to contribute something to our knowledge of reality in the world of *Don Quixote*. Some may think that certain of our examples are not to be taken seriously, because they belong to the counterfeit adventures. Such does not seem to be Cervantes' notion. In the world he created, "practical jokes are turned to earnest" (II. 49), and not only is it hard to distinguish feigned realities from true ones, but the former prove just as efficacious as the latter. This idea is expressed with absolute clarity at the end of the tragic story of *The Man Too Curious for His Own Good:* "Anselmo had been most attentive listening and seeing the tragedy of his honor's death, which was *represented* with such rare and moving passion by the actors in it that it *seemed* that what they *feigned* had been transformed into the *truth* itself" (I. 34).

15. Years ago Amédée Mas wrote some interesting comments about the theme of reality. Among them we find: "On the other hand, perhaps it is not useless to emphasize that what is variable, oscillating, undulating, changeable for Cervantes are, the images, the representations of reality, not reality itself." See his "Le Thème de la réalité oscillante dans Don Quichotte," in *Hommage à Ernest Martinenche* (Paris, n.d.), pp. 375-380. But if reality can be represented in so many ways and presented in such varied images, and if it is so difficult for everybody, including the narrator, to cope with, don't these facts themselves say something about the nature of reality?

5 · ILLUSIONS

*I*T IS NOT A SIMPLE matter to cope with the world as it is portrayed in *Don Quixote*. In it we have noted situations and happenings difficult to interpret—so difficult, indeed, that man may be driven to enchantment to explain them. We have perceived that reality often wears a look of confusion and is usually open to more than one interpretation; also that practical jokes are turned to earnest, that lies may appear to be truths, and that the truth itself may deceive. In sum, we have observed that all this, although corresponding more to the experience of Don Quixote and Sancho Panza than to that of the other characters, may also be extended to these. Now, as we try to delve deeper into the psychic zone of the quixotic world, we will discover the problems and perplexities of that world reflected in an attitude observable in all the characters and expressed in the novel literally hundreds of times.[1]

The attitude referred to above is one of surprise, wonder, astonishment, amazement, even awe. Every degree imaginable within this series is expressed. The word most frequently used by Cervantes is *admirar(se)* and its derivatives. Also used with frequency are *suspender(se)*, *maravillarse*, *espantarse*, and their derivatives. And all these words are used either alone or combined with other analogous words.[2] From here on they are translated into English and printed in italics.

1. The vocabulary studied in this chapter abounds also in the pastoral novel, because it, too, concerns itself with the psychic life of man, as has been noted more than once. One of the novelties of *Don Quixote* is that this life is given a more believable setting.

2. It would be difficult to give a carefully nuanced translation of all of these combinations, but here are some chosen to reveal the variety to be

We already know that the image the world offered to Don Quixote and Sancho did not always coincide with the one they carried in their heads. A study of the vocabulary mentioned above reveals that to a surprising extent the same thing can be said of the other characters in the novel. The astonishment they so often express bears witness to it. A few of the many examples that might be adduced are exhibited in the following paragraph.

As he tells Don Quixote and Sancho what he knows about the unknown madman, the goatherd of Sierra Morena says, among other things: "And being in the best part of his story, he stopped and fell silent; he fixed his eyes on the ground for a while, during which we were all quiet and *perplexed*, waiting to see how that trance would end" (I. 23). Of his final interview with Luscinda, Cardenio speaks in these terms: "she wept, moaned, and sighed, and went off, and left me full of *confusion* and *fright*, *astounded* to have seen such new and such sad signs of sorrow and regret in Luscinda" (I. 27). The narrator relates how Lothario receives the money with which to tempt Camila: "The next day I received the four thousand crowns, and with them four thousand *confusions*" (I. 33). Camila does not understand the conduct of her husband: "Camila was *surprised* at Anselmo's answer, which filled her with more *confusion* than before" (I. 34). Lothario suggests to Anselmo that his wife's fortitude is at last overcome: "At Lothario's words Anselmo remained *absorbed*, *bewildered* and *full*

---

found in the novel: *admirarse y suspenderse; admirar, suspender, alborozar y entretener; admirar y espantar; admirados, pasmados, atónitos; absorto, suspenso y admirado; confusión y espanto; confuso y pensativo; confuso y temoroso; confusos y alegres; desesperado y confuso; suspensos y atónitos; suspenso y maravillado; suspenso, confuso y admirado; mudos y suspensos; suspenso y asombrado; suspenso y colérico; dudosos y suspensos; quedos y suspensos; encantar y suspender; maravillar y suspender; atónito y pasmado; pasmado . . . absorto . . . suspenso . . . atónito . . . abobado . . . confuso . . . espantado.* The specialist who wants to know the page on which each of these combinations appears may consult p. 114 of the Spanish edition of this study.

of wonder" (I. 34). Don Quixote becomes angry with Sancho because of what he had said about Dorotea and the giant: "Didn't you just now tell me that this princess had turned into a damsel called Dorotea and that the head which I understand I cut off a giant was the bitch that bore you along with other bits of nonsense that put me into the greatest *confusion* I have ever experienced in all the days of my life?" (I. 37). When Don Luis had finished the story of his falling in love, the judge was "*bewildered, confused,* and *surprised*" (I. 44). When the Priest and the Bachelor had read the letters received by Teresa Panza, "they looked at each other as though *full of wonder* at what they had read" (II. 50). After the Priest had examined and certified the fineness of the coral necklace, "he was again filled with *wonder*" (II. 50). Frequently, the astonishment expressed by the narrator is collective. Here is how he expresses the reaction of all those who witnessed Master Peter's reception of Don Quixote: "Don Quixote was *dumbfounded*, Sancho *absorbed*, the cousin *perplexed*, the page *aghast*, the fellow from the braying town *stupefied*, the innkeeper *confused*, and, in short, all who heard the words of the puppeteer were *astonished*" (II. 25). When Countess Trifaldi and her duennas revealed their beards, "the Duke and Duchess showed themselves *full of wonder*, Don Quixote and Sancho were *dumbfounded*, and all present were *aghast*" (II. 39). Before Governor Sancho delivered his judgment in the case of alleged rape, the author tells his readers: "All those present were *perplexed*, awaiting the outcome of that dispute" (II. 45). On his nocturnal patrol Sancho and his entourage stumbled upon a pretty little damsel. Here is the author's account of their reaction: "Finally, the lass looked good to all of them, and none of those who saw her knew her, and the natives of the town said they could not imagine who she might be, and those who were in on the jokes being played on Sancho were the most *surprised* of all, because that meeting had not been contrived by them, and thus they were *in doubt*, awaiting the outcome of the case" (II. 49). In the episode of the enchanted head, the narrator describes the growing wonder of all those present, even those who were in on the prank: "and if Don Antonio had not first revealed the secret to his friends, they too would have fallen into the same *wondering surprise* as all the rest. . . . Hearing which, all were *aghast*. . . . Now indeed was everyone *surprised* again, now indeed did everyone's hair stand on end with pure *fright*" (II. 62).

What is it that so frequently surprises the inhabitants of the world of *Don Quixote?* Simply everything: the appearances of their world, the situations they fall into, and, above all, the conduct of the people they encounter. When we studied the words *seem* and *must*, we saw how difficult it is to know people and to interpret, much less anticipate, what they may take a notion to say or do. This may not seem extraordinary in the case of extraordinary people such as Don Quixote and Sancho, but it is striking to note that supposedly sane people who have known each other long and intimately may still spring large and unpleasant surprises on one another. Consider the two friends in the story of *The Man Too Curious for His Own Good.* After listening attentively to the words of his friend, "Lothario remained looking at him for a good while, as though he were looking at something he had never seen before and which caused him *wonder* and *fright*." Finally, Lothario speaks: "Without doubt I imagine either that you don't know me or I don't know you" (I. 33). At bottom, man is a mystery, and God alone knows what he is capable of at any given moment. Sancho said it very well when the squire of the Knight of the Wood tried to incite him to battle: "The wisest course would be to let everybody's anger sleep; 'cause no one knows another's soul, and he who is wont to come for wool may go away shorn; and God blessed peace and cursed quarrels; because if a cat, cornered and hard pressed, turns into a lion, God knows what I, who am a man, may turn into" (II. 14).

Man's conduct may appear strange for many reasons, not the least of which is his propensity to disregard reality the better to nurture the illusions he is forever forging. *Don Quixote* overflows with illustrations of this propensity, and they are worth studying. We may begin by seeking the motives that push men to irrational conduct. In this respect, we will say little of Don Quixote here, since the whole next chapter is devoted to him.

Man scarcely needs a springboard to dive into the wish-fulfilling waters of illusion. Take Sancho for example. While Don Quixote remains in Sierra Morena doing penance, Sancho sets out to carry a message to Dulcinea. On the way he encounters the Priest and the Barber to whom he says, among other things, "that when he had brought a favorable reply from Dulcinea, his master was going to set about trying to be an emperor or, at least, a monarch; for so they had planned it between them, and it was a simple thing for him to become one in view of the valor of his person and the strength of his arm; and when he was, he would marry his squire, who by then couldn't fail to be a widower, and he would give him to wife one of the Empress' ladies in waiting, the heiress to a rich and large estate on dry land without any islands, which he no longer wanted" (I. 26). This illusion originates in the promise of an island, despite what Sancho has just said about islands. If Sancho has faith in his master, he may believe in the possible reality of this kind of reward for faithful service, but what grounds can he have for believing in the timely widowerhood to which he has just alluded? Not long afterward the power of this same illusory reward prompts Sancho to draw an imprudent comparison between Dul-

cinea and Princess Micomicona, and this earns him a couple
of blows from his master that nearly leave him incapacitated
for further illusions (I. 30). A little later the same illusion
blinds him to the reality of the wineskins pierced by his
master's sword (I. 35). Before the third sally, the same illusion gives rise to a quarrel between Sancho and his wife
over the future marriage of their daughter (II. 5). Finally,
the same illusion provides a basis for Teresa Panza and her
daughter to imagine themselves countesses driving through
the streets of the Court in a carriage (II. 50).

It should be noted that materialistic interests are not the
only ones that move Sancho to behave so irrationally. Like
his master, he too is sensitive to the prick of fame: "I, Master Sansón, intend to seek fame not as a valiant warrior
but as the best and most loyal squire that ever served knight-
errant" (II. 4; also II. 8, 34). Here we need not exhaust the
motives that make Sancho persist in the mad adventure of
following and serving a madman; let us, rather, recall the
noble words with which he tried to satisfy some of the
doubts of the Duchess; they reveal a side of Sancho not well
represented by the previous quotations: "I recognize the
truth of what you say: if I were discreet, I would have
left my master days ago. But this was my fate, and this
my misfortune; I cannot help it; follow him I must: we are
from the same village, I have eaten his bread, I like him
well, he is grateful, he gave me his donkeys, and, above all,
I am faithful; and so it is impossible that we can be separated by any event but that of the final digging" (II.
33).

At times it is their passions that blind men to reality. As
we noted in an earlier chapter, Don Quixote believes that
fear disturbs Sancho's senses and prevents him from seeing
things aright. Fear is a major factor in Cardenio's unhappy
life, and we will come back to it later. Another powerful
passion is that of vengeance. In *Don Quixote* there are at

least four persons whose irrational conduct can be explained wholly or in part by the desire to avenge themselves. After seeing the hasty departure of Leonela's lover, Lothario was dying "to take revenge on Camila" (I. 34). The Captive speaks of a European renegade (Uchalí) who, "to seek vengeance, gave up his faith" (I. 40). Many pages back we noticed that what led Sansón Carrasco to follow Don Quixote a second time was not "the desire that he recover his sanity but the desire for revenge" (II. 15). Finally, Roque Guinart confesses that in his disordered life vengeance has played the decisive role: "I have been led into it [his way of life] by I know not what desires for revenge, which have the power to disturb the calmest spirits" (II. 60).

The passion of love is another great upsetter of rational conduct. How many characters refer to its power and its effects! Vivaldo, for example, speaks of the "end to which come all those who plunge down the path that unbridled love sets before their eyes" (I. 13). Leonela speaks of the "snare of love" (I. 34); Lothario, of "so powerful an enemy as love" (I. 34); Altisidora, of "the powerful force of love" (II. 44). Referring to the love affair of Lothario and Camila, the narrator affirms: "the passion of love is overcome only by flight; let no one test his mettle with so powerful an enemy, because divine strength is needed to conquer its human strength" (I. 34). Don Quixote, who began to speak of the "amorous pestilence" in his discourse on the Golden Age, treats of it again and again: "love and liking blind the eyes of understanding" (II. 19); "the power of love is wont to unhinge the soul" (II. 46). And, of course, one can scarcely turn to love without finding jealousy, perhaps the most destructive of all the passions.[3]

3. Here we might recall in passing that out of feigned love real pique may emerge. Altisidora furnishes a good example as she shouts at Don Quixote, "By the Lord, Don Codfish, Soul of Lead, Date Pit, more

Cardenio's madness was due in large part to jealousy. Here is how he describes his state of mind on hearing Luscinda's ill-fated *yes:* "I was left without counsel; foresaken, it seemed, by heaven itself; converted into an enemy of the earth that sustained me; the air denying me breath for my sighs; the water, humor for my eyes; only the fire increased, so that I burned all over with rage and jealousy" (I. 27). If, as we have noted, Lothario was dying to take revenge on Camila, it was because he was "blind with the jealous rage that gnawed his guts" (I. 34). Afterward he realizes his mistake and the fact that, "instigated by the furious rage of jealousy," he has gotten himself into "so tangled a labyrinth" (I. 34). Claudia Jerónima also comes to understand the tragic outcome of her love affair: "Oh raging power of jealousy, to what a desperate end do you conduct those who admit you to their busom" (II. 60). And the narrator emphasizes the point: "But, what else could be expected, if the harsh and invincible power of jealousy wove the fabric of their lamentable story?" (II. 60). Actually, it matters little whether or not jealousy has a sufficient cause. Imagined jealousy is hardly distinguishable from the authentic variety: "And thus did imagined jealousy and dreaded suspicion fatigue Grisóstomo as though they were true" (I. 14). We find a collective example in the story of Leandra: "To all, the madness extended to such degree that some complained of her disdain who had never spoken to her and even lamented and suffered the raging sickness of jealousy, which she gave to no one; because, as I have already said, her sin was discovered before her desire" (I. 51).

Perhaps nothing feeds illusion so much as imagination. The verb *to imagine* (and its derivatives) figures with

---

obstinate and hard-hearted than a peasant begged to change his mind; if I get at you, I'll scratch your eyes out! Do you think, Don Vanquished and Beaten to a Pulp, that I died because of you. Everything you have seen this night was feigned" (II. 70).

notable frequency in Cervantes' masterpiece, and often appears in the company of other words suggesting the role they play in the process of illusion: "disordered imaginings" (I. 29), "mad imagining" (I. 42), "confused imagination" (I. 46), "labyrinth of imaginings" (I. 48), "wrapt and entangled in these and many other imaginings" (II. 3). Sancho becomes angry with Dulcinea's imagined negative response before he ever undertakes his never-accomplished mission to her: " 'cause if she doesn't answer the way she should, I swear to whom I may that I'll get a favorable reply out of her guts by kicks and blows. Because, how are we to endure that so famous a knight-errant as your grace should go needlessly mad on account of a ——? I hope the lady won't make me come out with it" (I. 25). Even Don Quixote realizes how rootless is Sancho's annoyance: "So Sancho ... it appears that you're no saner than I am" (I. 25). Sancho poses and resolves the problem of imagined Negro vassals on the yet-to-be-won estates of his master: "the only thing that troubled him was to think that that kingdom was in the land of the Negroes and that the people they might give him as vassals would all be Negroes; for which he contrived a good remedy in his imagination" (I. 29). Part of Cardenio's misfortune is due to imagined fears: "I left sad and pensive, my soul full of imaginings and suspicions, without knowing what I suspected or imagined" (I. 27). He had already alluded to the part imagination played in his madness: "it is evident to me that the strong imagination of my misfortunes is so intense and is so powerful in my destruction that, without my being able to prevent it, I remain as though of stone, lacking all good sense and understanding" (I. 27). Dorotea turned over in her imagination Fernando's demands (I. 28), and after her seduction, left her house accompanied by her servant and "many imaginings" (I. 28). When Tomé Cecial abandoned him, Sansón Carrasco "remained behind imagining his revenge" (II. 15). Thoughts and imaginings kill Anselmo. After leaving his home and city for the last time, we are told that, "harassed by his thoughts," he had to dismount and rest. Having arrived at the house of his friend and "seeing himself, then, alone, the imagination of his misfortune began to weigh so heavily upon him that he clearly recognized his life was coming to an end" (I. 35).

The first paragraph of chapter 40, Part II, is dedicated by Cervantes to praise of Cide Hamete Benegeli's narrative art. In spite of its obvious irony, it does call attention to an essential feature of that art: "He paints thoughts, uncovers imaginings, answers unasked questions, clarifies doubts." That is to say, he takes pains to reveal the inner life of his characters and to underscore its vital importance. We have already seen this clearly manifested through Cervantes' frequent use of such words as *imagination*. Another word of similar use is *thought*. In *Don Quixote* there abound phrases like "entranced and carried away by his thoughts" (I. 12), "these thoughts led him so much out of himself" (II. 11), "A heavy load of thoughts and discomforts" (II. 13), "buried in his thoughts" (II. 30), "wrapt in his thoughts" (II. 46). Don Quixote owes his knightly existence to "the strangest thought that madman ever had" (I. 1). If the Priest and the Barber despaired of his mental health, it was because they observed "how intent he was on his disordered thoughts" (II. 2). And these thoughts may count for life and death: "if it were not for the extraordinary thoughts of Don Quixote, who took it into his head that the Bachelor was not the Bachelor, Sir Bachelor would have remained forever incapacitated for attaining the Master's degree" (II. 15). The battle between Don Quixote and Tosilos never came off because the latter "had other thoughts" (II. 56) than those of the Duke. Tosilos wanted to get married without fighting the Knight of the Sad Countenance, but he finally had to confess: "it turned out quite the reverse of my thought" (II. 66)—and this, because he failed to take into account the Duke's thinking. Lothario understands that the life of a person may be determined by that person's thoughts: "he decided to satisfy him [Anselmo] and do what he asked, with the purpose and intention of guiding that business in such a way that, without disturbing Camila's thoughts, Anselmo would be satisfied" (II. 33). We already know the tragic happenings that came about when Camila's thoughts were finally disturbed. To a degree, man is what he thinks he is or what he is thought to be. About what people say of her, Dorotea complains in these terms: "and I heard people were saying that I had been taken from the house of my parents by the servant lad who came with me, something which hurt me deeply, because it showed how low my credit had fallen, since it was not enough to lose it with my journey, without saying with whom, his being so low a fellow and so unworthy of my good thoughts" (I. 28). In praising his older brother, the Judge refers to him as "stronger and of higher thoughts than I" (I. 42). One might almost say that a man's thoughts are his life. Don Quixote speaks more than once in such terms. For example, in reference to the diabolical invention of artillery, he says, "a stray missile arrives . . . and cuts short and ends in an instant the thoughts and life of one who deserved to enjoy life for long centuries" (II. 38). The night that Don Quixote tried to whip Sancho, the latter made him promise not to touch him again: "Don Quixote promised and swore by the life of his thoughts not to touch a thread of his clothing" (II. 60).

Everybody tends to give free rein to his thoughts and imaginings; that is, everybody tends to live in a world of his own, where what is needed is promptly invented.[4] One of the things most needed by man is hope, which often rests

<hr>

4. In one of his recent essays on *Don Quixote*, Américo Castro says: "After the fashion of Cervantes, everything is as man makes it be, whether to his peril or to his advantage." See his *El ingenioso hidalgo*, p. xix.

more firmly on the will of him who needs it than on the true circumstances of his life. Thus, in the middle of her story, we hear Dorotea say: "All these things I turned over in my fancy, and I consoled myself without having any consolation, feigning faint and distant hopes to prolong the life that I abhor" (I. 28). The narrator tells us that for some time Camila turned her back on Lothario's amorous advances. "But hope did not grow faint in Lothario because of this coldness, for hope is always born with love" (I. 33). The Captive also sustained himself with unfounded hopes: "Never did the hope of getting free abandon me; and when, in what I devised, thought, and put into action, the outcome did not correspond to my intention, then, without giving up, I sought and feigned another hope to sustain me, however weak and feeble it might be" (I. 40). On hearing Sancho speak of the hardships of squires, the Squire of the Wood remarks: "All that can be borne . . . with the hope we have of reward" (II. 13). Shortly thereafter, Sancho admits the illusory character of the hopes that incite him to continue in the "dangerous occupation of squire, into which I have fallen a second time, lured and deceived by a purse with a hundred crowns which I found one day in the heart of Sierra Morena, and the devil puts before my eyes here, there, and everywhere a sack full of doubloons, which, it seems to me, with every step, I touch, embrace, and carry home, and invest, and get income, and live like a prince; and all the while I am thinking about this, I find easy and bearable the labors I endure with this fool of a master, who is more of a madman than a knight" (II. 13).

Sancho is not the only one who refuses to heed the voice of reason. Many other characters do likewise. Aside from Don Quixote, who furnishes the best example of this kind of willfulness, Cardenio is the first character, following the chronology of the novel, whom we should consider in this connection. Here are the words that testify to his irrational willfulness: "and don't tire yourselves persuading me or advising me what reason tells you may be good for my recovery . . . I do not want health without Luscinda" (I. 27). Anselmo makes a similar confession: "and likewise I see and confess that if I do not follow your opinion and if I do follow my own, I will be fleeing from good and running after evil" (I. 33). Although he nowhere expresses it so clearly as Anselmo, Lotario too recognizes that his conduct defies prudence. Another who knows himself led down the path of evil is Roque Guinart. Although Don Quixote has not asked him for explanations, Roque feels impelled to explain his strange life: "as I have said, the will to avenge myself for a wrong that was done me so overthrows all my good inclinations that I persist in this state in spite of what I understand; and as one abyss calls to another, and one sin to another sin, my revenges have formed a chain so that not only my own but those of others do I take upon myself, but God is pleased that, even though I see myself in the middle of the labyrinth of my confusion, I do not lose hope of reaching a safe harbor" (II. 60). With the exception of Roque, all the characters mentioned in this chapter are called or call themselves mad.[5] The same may be said of Sancho.[6] As for Roque Guinart, who knows himself to be off the road of reason and lost in a labyrinth of confusion, Don Quixote diagnoses his ailment as "sickness of his conscience" (II. 60). In the world of *Don Quixote* willful perseverance in irrational behavior is seen as a sign of insanity.

There are other characters, as well, who have had at least a brush with madness. We know that the desire for vengeance holds Sansón Carrasco to his lunacy despite the warning of his squire (II. 15). The narrator directs our attention to a curious quirk in Don Lorenzo's behavior: "Isn't it rich that they say Don Lorenzo was much pleased at Don

5. For Cardenio see I. 23, 24, 27; for Anselmo, I. 33 (repeatedly), 35; for Lotario, I. 34.
6. See I. 25, 35; II. 7, 32.

Quixote's praise, even though he took him for a madman?" (II. 18). There is the collective madness of the braying town where "many times the mocked, armed and in formation, have sallied forth to do battle with their mockers, without king or rook, fear or shame, being able to prevent it" (II. 25). About the Duke and the Duchess, Cide Hamete says: "as far as he is concerned, the mockers are as mad as the mocked, and the Duke and the Duchess came within an inch of appearing fools themselves, since they took such pains to make fun of two fools" (II. 70).[7] And those who are not crazy may appear to be so: Luscinda "appeared like a person out of her mind" (I. 36); Don Luis "showed signs of going crazy" (I. 43); Basilio "ever walks pensive and sad, talking to himself, thereby giving clear and certain signs of losing his mind" (II. 19).

In brief, what can we say about the style of living shown by those who represent the society in which Don Quixote undertakes his quest? Well, they tend to live in a world of their own, made of imaginings, thoughts, desires, and hopes. Often they are astonished to see that the realities of the alien world differ so gravely from those of their personal world, but the discrepancies they find rarely affect their illusions. Even when they are aware that their behavior is irrational, they may persist in it, and this persistence may lead to madness. Of course, we must not exaggerate the volume of lunacy that hovers over Don Quixote's world. It is true that most of its inhabitants are not mad, but it is also true that even the sanest may sometimes wander near the brink of potential madness.[8]

7. See also II. 32 for the Chaplain's view of the Duke and Duchess.

8. I have found in Cervantes' characters something of what Américo Castro has found in the Hispanic style of life. The curious reader may verify this similarity by reading the last chapter of his *Structure of Spanish History* (Princeton University Press, 1954), in which Castro insists on the importance of will, fantasy, disregard of the reality of the intelligible world, withdrawal into a personal world, etc. Here is a summarizing sample: "In opposition to the principle inherited from Greece that reality 'is what it is,' the Spaniard sustained the principle that reality was what he felt, believed, and imagined" (p 613).

6 · MADNESS AND RECOVERED SANITY

*C*ERVANTES BEGINS and ends his masterpiece by saying that he wrote it to "destroy the authority and acceptance that the books of chivalry have in the world and among the common people" (I. Prologue). That is to say, he announces his book as a parody. If his hero goes crazy reading the nonsensical books of chivalry, this fact seems to convert his madness into the principal instrument of parody.[1] Observing this permits us to formulate a question that, formulated or not, has disturbed many readers. The question is, Is it possible to present madness as authentic human experience and at the same time make it serve the ends of parody? Many readers seem to think not. Some tend to accept the parody and reject the madness; others, to accept the madness and reject the parody.[2] The second tendency is the currently prevailing one, although the function

1. While there are all kinds of references to the interpretation of Don Quixote's madness that are of possible interest, I will mention only two: Otis H. Green, "El ingenioso hidalgo," *Hispanic Review*, 25 (1957), 175-193; and Robert Lindner, "The Jet-Propelled Couch," *Harper's Magazine* (December 1954, January 1955). Green's article demonstrates how the subject of this chapter is illuminated by the physiological and psychological ideas of a sixteenth-century Spanish doctor, Huarte de San Juan. Robert Lindner, a well-known psychoanalyst, reports a contemporary case which shows suggestive similarities to that of Don Quixote.
2. In speaking of reader reaction, I am thinking chiefly not of critics and scholars but of readers like my students, for example. They tend to accept Don Quixote's madness, but without believing in it deeply. Some thirty years ago Thomas Mann wrote an essay on *Don Quixote* which shows that everything about the novel delighted him except the ending. He concludes that Cervantes rendered a satisfactory ending impossible by making us love his mad hero while using his madness as an instrument of parody. This seems to be what disturbs some of my students. For Mann's ideas see his "A Bordo con Don Quijote," *Revista de Occidente*, 48 (1935), 184-186.

that madness seems to serve in the novel still bothers some of the readers inclined to take that madness as genuine. Without denying that the novel is in part parody, we shall deliberately ignore it for a while and see how Don Quixote's madness impresses us if we take it seriously.

For the modern reader to accept wholeheartedly Don Quixote's madness, it is necessary for him to know what drove Don Quixote to read so excessively in the literature of chivalry that he unhinged his mind. As Cervantes does not reveal the cause, the reader has to imagine it for himself. Azorín, for whom the total environment of La Mancha helps to explain the knight's madness, writes: "Tell me, do you not understand in these lands the dreams, the whims, the unbridled imaginings of the great madman? Fantasy springs to frantic flight over these plains; in the brain arise visions, chimeras, insane and tormenting fancies." [3] As suggested by Castro, another point of view from which to understand Don Quixote's escape from the humdrum world of his day may be found in these words of Friar Alonso de Cabrera, preacher to Philip II: "Our grandfathers, my lords, lamented the winning of Granada from the Moors, because on that day the horses fell lame and the cuirasses and lances began to rust, and the shields to rot. And the distinguished cavalry of Andalusia was finished, and it was the end of youth and all its well-known gallantries." [4] Azorín and Castro are not the only ones who have imagined such amplifications of the Cervantine text; but the most telling evidence may be found in the novel itself.

In the first pages Cervantes gives us what little certain knowledge we have of the process by which his hero went mad. We learn that he was idle most of the year and that he filled his idle hours with such immoderate readings of chivalric romances "that he spent his night's reading from

3. *La Ruta de Don Quijote* (3d ed. Madrid, 1915), p. 183.
4. In Castro, *Structure of Spanish History*, pp. 612-613.

twilight to dawn and his days from daybreak to nightfall;
and so, from little sleeping and much reading, his brain
dried up and he lost his mind" (I. 1).[5] Then we are told that
he filled his fancy with all the deeds and ceremonies of
knighthood and that he came to believe in them as though
they were the truth itself. Having lost his mind and filled
his fancy with such nonsense, "he hit upon the strangest
thought that madman ever had in this world, and it was that
it seemed to him fitting and necessary, both for the increase
of his own honor and for the service of the republic, to become a knight-errant and to wander through the world
with horse and armor in search of adventures" (I. 1).

The Manchegan gentleman goes crazy from reading too
many books of chivalry, and from the beginning his madness is tied tightly and exclusively to his vision of knighthood.[6] Having decided to put into effect his "strange
thought," he begins at once to take the steps required for
him to be able to consider himself a knight. One of these
steps is material: to find and refurbish the necessary knightly gear. The others are mental: to select a new name for
himself and for his nag, and to find and name a lady with
whom to fall in love. That is, he tries to rearrange his familiar world so that it can accommodate his madness.[7]

5. Antonio Vilanova believes that Cervantes found in Erasmus the
idea that too little sleep and excessive reading were responsible for Don
Quixote's madness. See his *Erasmo y Cervantes* (Barcelona, 1949), p.
47.
6. The reader probably remembers how frequently the novel records
the notion that Don Quixote "is mad in streaks, full of lucid intervals"
(II. 18), and that his spells of insanity are always associated with his
knightly impulses. Cervantes emphasizes this notion by reminding the
reader how often it is expressed in his novel: "But, as has been often
said in the progress of this great history, he only talked nonsense when
the subject of chivalry was broached, and in his other discourse he
showed a clear and free understanding, so that at every turn his actions
discredited his judgment, and his judgment, his actions" (II. 43).
7. Among these first steps we may include exercises in the use of
chivalric language. After revealing to us the thoughts with which the
novel knight entertained himself on the morning of his first sally, the

What concept of chivalry did Don Quixote hold? To begin with, he decided not only to become a knight and sally forth in search of adventures, but "to practice everything he had read that knights practiced, righting all manner of wrongs and exposing himself to occasions and dangers, by overcoming which he might win eternal name and fame" (II. 1). As a start, then, we may say that he sought a profession in which to help people in distress and to win lasting fame for himself. As he rides forth for the first time, he is thinking of his future fame and of Dulcinea, without whom he cannot be regarded as a genuine knight, because "a knight-errant without a lady is like a tree without leaves, a building without a foundation, and a shadow without a body to cast it" (II. 32). Totally indispensable to his concept of chivalry is this lady, without whom, and "if it were not for the valor with which she endows my arm, I wouldn't have enough to kill a flea" (I. 30). She inspires and enlightens him, because "any ray that from the sun of her beauty reaches my eyes will illuminate my understanding and fortify my heart, so that I may become unique and peerless in discretion and courage" (II. 8). To her he wishes to attribute all his glory and fame, because "all that I have achieved, do achieve, or may achieve by arms in this life comes to me from the favor she gives me and from my being hers" (I. 31). Without Dulcinea how could Don Quixote continue to believe himself a knight?

On the basis of what we have so far recorded, we may say that Don Quixote's chivalric ideal consists of three essential parts: to serve a great lady, to seek good fame, and to succor the oppressed and the needy. For him all three are imbued with the spirit of religion. Before the adventure with Andrés, Don Quixote was explaining to Sancho how

---

author makes the following comment: "He was stringing together like beads these and other pieces of nonsense, all in the style that his books of chivalry had taught him, imitating as well as he could their language" (I. 2).

knights serve their ladies: "Because you must know that in this our style of chivalry it is a great honor for a lady to have many knights to serve her, without their thoughts extending beyond serving her because of who she is, without expecting any reward for their many good desires except that she be pleased to accept them as her knights" (I. 31). Sancho grasps at once the religious character of such love: "With this kind of love," said Sancho, "I have heard it preached that we should love our Lord, for Himself alone, without our being moved by hope of glory or fear of punishment" (I. 31).

As to good fame, Don Quixote has a program for its attainment. Talking to Sancho on the road to El Toboso, he says,

> Thus, O Sancho, our deeds must not overreach the limits fixed for us by the Christian religion which we profess. We should slay haughtiness by slaying giants; slay envy by our generosity and good heart; wrath by our serene bearing and quiet spirit; gluttony and sleep by eating little and holding nightly vigil; lust and lasciviousness by keeping faith with those we have made the mistresses of our thoughts; sloth by traveling the whole world over, seeking opportunities that may and will make us famous knights as well as Christians. You see here, Sancho, the means by which one may gain the highest praise which good fame brings with it [II. 8].

Don Quixote never forgets that whatever he undertakes in pursuit of fame must be subordinated to the divine will. Speaking to Vivaldo about the profession of knights-errant, he affirms that they are the agents of God: "Thus we are the ministers of God on earth and the arms by which His justice is carried out" (I. 13). How many times he reaffirms the idea of dependence on divine will that he expressed to Sancho in the adventure of the fulling mills:

"I was born, by Heaven's will, in this iron age of ours to restore the age of gold" (I. 20).[8] His mission is God-given, and he acts in His name. Thus does he express himself as he accepts the responsibility for rescuing Princess Micomicona: "Let us depart from here in the name of God to favor that great lady" (I. 29). To fulfill his divine mission, he freed the galley slaves, and that is the ground on which he stands when he is criticized for doing it: "I came across a string of sad and unfortunate people, and I did for them what my religion requires of me, and let the rest take care of itself" (I. 30). Shortly after formulating his already cited program for winning good fame, he repeats that knighthood is a religion. Sancho has just proposed that they go in for sainthood to achieve good fame. His master replies, "But we can't all be friars, and many are the paths by which God calls His own to Heaven; knighthood is a religion; there are sainted knights in Heaven" (II. 8).

If knighthood is a religion, then to be knighted may produce effects similar to those of a religious conversion. In his dispute with the Canon of Toledo over books of chivalry, Don Quixote says, "Of myself I can say that since I have been a knight-errant, I am brave, courteous, liberal, well-bred, generous, polite, bold, gentle, patient, and able to endure labors, imprisonments, enchantments" (I. 50). And he tries to extend some of these effects to his squire: "As far as I can tell, you are clearly a blockhead who, without rising early or staying up late or doing anything at all, with merely the breath of chivalry which has touched you, has become without more ado the governor of an island, as though that were a trifle" (II. 42).

Don Quixote's view of knighthood as being both military

8. Other examples attributing his mission to divine will: "the effect for which Heaven hurled me into the world" (I. 49); "I was born into the world to right such wrongs" (I. 52); "to whom is reserved by order of High Heaven the accomplishment of this adventure" (II. 29).

and religious corresponds well enough with some of the
medieval military and religious orders; and as we have seen,
he lays an extraordinary stress on the religious side. But
what, one may wonder, has all this to do with his madness?
We have already established the fact that Don Quixote's
madness is inseparably bound to chivalry and that the form
his madness takes requires him to become a knight-errant.
Also, we have had occasion to observe that in the long run
the modern world is hostile to knight-errantry and, therefore, to him. And it is precisely to placate that hostility and
to win a measure of acceptance for his ideal that Don Quixote puts such emphasis on the noblest aspect of his unsea-
sonable profession. The Canon of Toledo tries to persuade
him that the numberless knights in which he believes have
never existed. To defend them and the order they professed,
our knight appeals to all kinds of argument, including that
of the ennobling effect of knighthood, which he has himself experienced. This is typical. When he is pressed the
hardest is the time he is most likely to stress the religious
side of his profession. A pair of examples will help to make
the point.

Before Don Quixote makes his third and final sally from
home, his housekeeper and niece try hard to dissuade him.
In the ensuing conversation the knight says,

> You will tire yourselves in vain persuading me that I
> should not want what the heavens want, what fortune
> orders and reason requires, and, above all, what my will
> desires; although knowing, as I do know, the innumer-
> able labors to which knight-errantry is subject, I also
> know the infinite good that can be attained through it;
> and I know that the path of virtue is very narrow and the
> road of vice broad and spacious; and I know that their
> ends and final resting-places are different; because that of
> vice, broad and spacious, ends in death, and that of virtue,

narrow and burdensome, ends in life, and not in life that ends but in life that shall have no end [II. 6].[9]

Perhaps it is the chaplain of the Duke and Duchess who attacks most harshly Don Quixote's chivalric pretensions. Although this time the tone of his defense may not be so religious as on some other already cited occasions, he does not fail to insist on the noble goals and high virtues he pursues:

I go by the narrow path of knighthood, to exercise which I disdain my estate but not my honor. I have satisfied wrongs, righted injustices, punished insolence, conquered giants, and trampled monsters under foot; I am in love, but only because knights must be in love; and being so, I am not of the licentious kind but of those who are restrained and platonic. My intentions are always directed to worthy ends, which are to do good to all and evil to none: if he who understands this, if he who performs these works, if he who deals in these things deserves to be called a simpleton, let your excellencies, Duke and Duchess, say so [II. 32].

Don Quixote needs to believe in knighthood and to win for it at least a minimum of acceptance by his contemporaries. In his vehement desire to achieve such acceptance and so justify in a measure his own illusions, he seeks a common

9. Compare Don Quixote's words with these words of Jesus: "Enter ye in by the narrow gate: for wide is the gate, and broad is the way, that leadeth to destruction, and many are they that enter in thereby. For narrow is the gate, and straightened the way, that leadeth unto life, and few are they that find it" (Matthew 7:13-14). It is not by mere chance that Don Quixote knows how to speak in words that echo the Bible; to be able to do so is for him part of the science of chivalry, as he said one day in Don Diego de Miranda's house: "he [a true knight] must be a theologian in order to know how to give a clear and distinct account of the Christian law he professes wherever it is asked for" (II. 18). Don Quixote uses this science to reason with the armed men from the braying town, and Sancho recognizes his competence: "the devil take me if this master of mine isn't a theologian" (II. 27).

ground, intelligible to him and to his contemporaries. In his search for an area of probable mutual agreement, he turns hopefully to that of high moral and religious ideals.

The elevated concept of chivalry held by Don Quixote is not the only bulwark for the defense of his knightly illusions. Above, in Chapter 3, we saw that enchantment served the same purpose. And his madness has still other defenses, which reveal better than anything else how intimate and imperious was our gentleman's need to see himself as a true knight. One of these defenses is the wise choice. For example, among the preparations undertaken by Don Quixote for his first sally, the reader will recall the repairing of his helmet. Once the repairs are made, he decides to test it with a couple of sword slashes. At the first blow the helmet falls apart. The gentleman repairs it once more, fortifying it with several iron bars. This time he declares it sound and chooses not to test it again, thus wisely eliminating the risk of disappointment.

Another example of wise choice can be found in the episode of Don Quixote's penance in Sierra Morena. The wild mountain scenes traversed by master and man seem to the former most suitable for doing penance, and he is not slow in remembering two cases from his beloved books: that of Amadis and that of Roland. He tells Sancho about them and announces his intention of remaining there alone to perform deeds as mad as theirs. Understanding that Don Quixote's models had cause for losing their minds, Sancho wants to know what Dulcinea has done to motivate such conduct in his master. The latter knows how to make merit of having no cause: "That's the fine point of my business; for a knight to turn mad with cause is nothing to celebrate: the real test is to do it without cause and let my lady know that if I do this in the dry, what would I do in the wet? What's more, I have ample occasion for madness in the long absence that has kept me from my lady Dulcinea del Toboso; because, as you heard that shepherd Ambrosio say some time ago, he who is absent suffers and fears every evil" (I. 25). Once Sancho has left on his mission to Dulcinea, Don Quixote ponders the two penances alluded to above. He remembers that Roland was driven to perform his wild deeds motivated by Angelica's infidelity, and he asks himself: "How can I imitate him in his madness, if I do not imitate him in its occasion?" (I. 26). And he understands that to do so would be to offend Dulcinea. It strikes him that Amadis' peaceful penance won him as great a lover's fame as anybody's. Therefore, he says, "If this is true, as it is, why should I now take the trouble to strip myself naked or bring to grief these trees which have done me no harm? Nor do I have cause to muddy the clear water of these streams, which will give me water to drink when I am thirsty. Long live the memory of Amadis, and let him be imitated by Don Quixote of La Mancha to the best of his ability" (I. 26). How many reasons his madness finds to imitate Amadis instead of Roland! In order to act like a knight-errant, he feels obliged to imitate one or the other. The most compelling reason for his imitation of Amadis' penance is that it is practicable while the other is not. Our knight recognizes this, too, although in an incidental kind of way: "Thus, it is easier for me to imitate him than to split giants in two, behead serpents, kill monsters, rout armies, break up armadas, and undo enchantments" (II. 25).

But not everything can be arranged by choosing the more feasible of two possible courses of action. Don Quixote runs into many troubles and suffers many misfortunes. How, for example, does he manage to continue seeing himself as an authentic knight-errant after he has received a furious beating at the hands of Galician packtrain carriers? The first thing it occurs to him to say is: "I should not have drawn sword against men who were not knights like myself; and so I believe that for having transgressed the laws of chivalry, the God of battles has permitted me to be given this punishment." A little later he adds, "and if it were not that I imagine—what do I mean imagine?—that I most certainly know that all these discomforts are part and parcel of the exercise of arms, I would let myself die on the spot out of sheer vexation." But still he can't recover his equanimity, and he continues to reflect on the indignity of his beating. He remembers that other famous knights suffered even worse indignities, and in thinking of them, he also remembers "that wounds given with whatever instruments happen to be at hand do not affront; and this is in the law of dueling, explicitly written." His personal dignity now somewhat restored, he addresses these concluding remarks to Sancho: "I say this so that you will not think that because we came out of this quarrel beaten to a pulp we received an affront, because the arms that those men carried, with which they pounded us, were nothing but staves, and none of them had, as far as I can remember, rapier, sword, or dagger" (I. 15).

We observed earlier that Don Quixote explains many misfortunes and difficulties as the work of evil enchanters, but we have not yet seen how slyly his madness can convert the confusion and anguish they produce into proof of knightly authenticity. When Sancho scolds him for continuing to call the barber's basin a helmet, his master answers with these words: "Is it possible that as long as you have traveled with me you have not noticed that all things associated with knights-errant seem to be chimeras, foolishness, and follies, that all are topsy-turvy? And not because it is really so, but because there always wander among us a swarm of enchanters who transform all our things and change them to their taste" (II. 25). What matters here is not merely that enchantment permits Don Quixote to go on believing that the basin is a helmet, but that to his canny madness the confused appearances are what is to be expected of "all things associated with knights-errant."

In Don Quixote's experience there are enchantments which depart from the usual style of enchantment. Enchanted knights "are generally carried through the air, with rare speed, enveloped in some gray and dark cloud, or on some chariot of fire, or mounted on some hippogriff or other similar beast" (I. 47). So it is that Don Quixote is filled with confusion to see himself borne away on an oxcart. How can he reconcile himself to this absurd transportation? Only by conjecturing that "perhaps the knight-errantry and enchantments of these times of ours must follow another road than in olden times. And also it might be that as I am a novel knight in the world, and the first to resuscitate the now forgotten exercise of adventurous knighthood, there may also have been invented new forms of enchantment and other ways of carrying off the enchanted" (I. 47).

Earlier we remarked that Don Quixote conducts the fantasies formed in the world of books through the real world of his contemporaries. We have seen that this world often shows itself inhospitable and incredulous. To escape from its doubts and jokes and pranks, he sometimes takes refuge again in the world of literature. It will be instructive to review several of these strategic retreats.

Shortly after the depressing adventure of the fulling mills, so bruising to Don Quixote's spirit and Sancho's flesh, the former acquires Mambrino's helmet. After this adventure they eat lunch, drinking from the stream that powered the mills, "without turning their faces toward them, such was the abhorrence in which they held them" (I. 21); then they depart. Whereupon Sancho begins to complain of the meager profits to be found by wandering about in such solitary places, where, even though they may perform great deeds, there is no one to see, know, or reward them. The squire proposes that they go and serve some emperor or noble prince. At once Don Quixote improvises the story of the "Knight-Errant." Like Don Quixote and Sancho, this imagined Knight has to make himself famous for his deeds before presenting himself at the court of the king, where he does finally arrive, carries several adventures to successful conclusion, wins the hand of the princess, and bestows favors on his squire.[10] If Don Quixote cannot satisfy Sancho with present realities, he can entertain him with pleasant fancies which allow him to forget for a while the insufficiencies of the real world.

When the Canon of Toledo tries to shake Don Quixote loose from his chivalric illusions, part of his response is to invent the story of the "Knight of the Lake" (I. 50).[11] To the Barber's impertinent and allusive story about the lunatic from Seville, part of his response is the diminutive story of the enchanted boat (II. 1).[12] When, on the road to El Toboso, Sancho insists that he saw Dulcinea winnowing wheat like a common peasant girl, his master flys away to the pastoral world of Garcilaso de la Vega: "Ill do you remember, O Sancho, those verses of our poet in which he paints for us the needlework done in their crystalline abodes by those four nymphs who emerged from the beloved river Tagus and sat in the green meadow to sew those rich fabrics that the ingenious poet describes for us, and which were all woven and interwoven with gold, silk, and pearls. And such must have been my lady's employment when you saw her" (II. 8).

On two occasions at least, Don Quixote satisfies temporarily his chivalric longings in dreams. The first occasion is the battle with the wineskins, which for our somnambulant

---

10. The story of the "Knight-Errant" foreshadows part of what is to occur later at the palace of the Duke and Duchess. Compare, for example, the second half of the story told by Don Quixote with the episode of Countess Trifaldi (II. 36). And of course it is at the palace of the Duke and Duchess that Sancho receives some of the favors he understands that squires are supposed to receive.

11. This knight's descent to the depths of the lake foreshadows Don Quixote's descent into the Cave of Montesinos (II. 22).

12. Subsequently Don Quixote has a similar adventure (II. 29).

knight represented the giant enemy of the Kingdom of Micomicón (I. 35). But the satisfaction of this victory is of short duration. The other occasion is the descent into the depths of the Cave of Montesinos, where Don Quixote finds a palace similar to the one found by the other knight at the bottom of the lake. There he meets two famous knights of old: Durandarte and Montesinos. The latter recognizes Don Quixote and tells him that for centuries they have been awaiting him, enchanted in those solitary depths. All of this goes very well with knight-errantry, but not everything witnessed there does. Out of keeping with the romances of chivalry is the capering of Dulcinea and her damsels, and especially the request of one of these to borrow a few coins for Dulcinea, using her skirt as security. On emerging from the Cave, Don Quixote relates what he has observed there. Since there are those who cannot believe his story, our knight himself soon develops doubts and anxieties. So keenly does he want to believe in this experience that he tries to make a pact with Sancho after the descent from their sky-ride on Clavileño: "Sancho, since you want people to believe what you saw in the sky, I want you to believe what I saw in the Cave of Montesinos. And I say no more" (II. 41).

In the long run, the interventions of friends and acquaintances in Don Quixote's life are fatal to his chivalric illusions, but in the beginning—and unintentionally—they help him to believe in them.[13] As we have seen, our knight desperately needs enchantment. Scarcely has he initiated his knightly career, when friends and family offer him convincing proof of its existence: the theft of his library by Freston (I. 7). Don Quixote yearns to succor damsels in

13. This is typical of the world of *Don Quixote*. We have said it before, but it is worth repeating. Once an action is launched, it follows its inevitable trajectory, but not for that reason does it fail to produce effects not foreseen by the launcher. Thus the world created by Cervantes seems ever charged with potentiality.

distress, and the Priest, with a different purpose in mind, helps him satisfy this desire by planning, with all the trappings of knight-errantry, an adventure with a damsel in distress (I. 26). But all this unintended and short-lived help does not free our knight from the necessity of defending his illusions heroically. And sometimes his only defense is his naked will. A few examples will show his use of this last-ditch defense.

What Don Quixote thinks sometimes has to be true simply because he says it is so. When Sancho reproaches him for his attack on the windmills, his master begins his usual explanation with these words: "all the more so because I believe, and such is the truth, that that magician Freston, who stole my room and books, has turned these giants into windmills to deprive me of the glory of their defeat" (I. 8). We know that it filled Don Quixote with confusion to be carried off in an oxcart, and have seen some of the reasoning he used to reconcile that bizarre transportation with genuine knightly enchantments. For a long while Sancho tries to get out of his master's head the notion that he is enchanted. Finally, the knight is left with no other shield than his willful need[14] to believe in his own enchantment: "I know and maintain that I am enchanted and that is enough for the security of my conscience, which would be greatly troubled if I thought I was not enchanted and allowed myself to remain in this cage like an idler and a coward, defrauding the many in need of the help and protection I might give them and which at this very hour they must urgently require" (I. 49). We have already cited the words with which Don Quixote conveys to his niece how useless it would be for her to try to dissuade him from sallying forth a third time on his noble mission; for he has to do "what the heavens want, what fortune orders, and

14. In his *El ingenioso hidalgo*, p. xxxv, Castro speaks of the "willful spontaneity" shown by Cervantes' characters.

reason requires, and, above all, what my will desires" (II. 6).

The illusion dearest to Don Quixote's heart is that of serving a great lady, and it was artful of his madness to take Dulcinea as his lady instead of Aldonza Lorenzo. So long as the latter remains hidden in Don Quixote's head, his zeal to exalt her need fear no hazard. We first realize this listening to Don Quixote's conversation with Vivaldo. The latter has asked him courteously about the name, country, rank, and beauty of his lady. Don Quixote answers, "Her name is Dulcinea; her country, El Toboso, a town of La Mancha; her rank must be at least that of princess, since she is my queen and mistress; her beauty, superhuman, since in her are realized all the impossible and chimerical attributes of beauty that poets give to their ladies." And the knight goes on detailing her many excellencies. When asked about her lineage, he enumerates the many famous families to which she does not belong and then concludes: "She belongs to those of El Toboso of La Mancha, a lineage which, although modern, is such that it may provide a generous beginning for the illustrious families of future centuries. And let no one contradict me" (I. 13).

When Don Quixote decides to send Sancho on a mission to Dulcinea, he commits an error which is to cost him dearly. Dulcinea is an admirable lady to serve from afar, but where can Sancho go with a letter but to the house of Aldonza Lorenzo? He remembers the latter as the robust peasant lass she is. Needless to say, Don Quixote is anything but pleased with the portrait his squire paints of her. Naturally, he cannot accept it and struggles to erase it with verbal ingenuities. At bottom, these rest on nothing but the will to believe, as his words testify: "and in final conclusion, I imagine that everything I say is so, with nothing lacking or in excess, and I paint her in my imagination as I desire her both in beauty and in rank; Helen is not her peer, nor is she rivaled by Lucretia or by any of the famous women of ancient times, whether Greek, Barbarian, or Roman" (I. 25).

When Sancho returns from his mission, his master asks him a series of questions about Dulcinea. All of his questions are so framed as to invite answers favorable to the exalted image of Dulcinea which he carries in his mind. The trouble is that Sancho does not cooperate. All of his answers tend to destroy that image. Not being disposed to tolerate that, Don Quixote ends up by leading the conversation away from Dulcinea. Here is a fragment of what he says, illustrating the willfulness with which our knight clings to his illusions: "Do you know what amazes me, Sancho? That you seem to have gone and returned through the air, having taken only a bit more than three days in going and coming from here to El Toboso, which is more than thirty leagues distant; by which circumstance I judge that wise necromancer who looks after my affairs and is my friend (because he is bound to exist, or else I wouldn't be a real knight-errant), I say, the aforesaid necromancer must have helped you on your way without your knowing it" (I. 31).

If it was already a mistake to send Sancho to see Dulcinea, even graver will be the mistake of Don Quixote's decision to go and see her himself; yet this is precisely what he determines to do. Master and man reach El Toboso at nightfall. For reasons not specified, the former postpones their entrance into the town until midnight. Once more the cunning of madness may be at work. The darkness of the night justifies somewhat their inability to find the nonexistent palace of Dulcinea, and they leave El Toboso, having agreed that Sancho will return by daylight to search for it. Knowing full well that to find it is impossible, Sancho decides to deceive his master by making him believe that three peasant girls who happen along later that day are Dulcinea and two of her damsels. Things turn out just as Sancho anticipated: Don Quixote attributes to evil enchanters the unimagined and uncouth appearance presented by Dulcinea. The knight is troubled and saddened by the ugly transmutation of his lady, and yet it saves him for a time from the danger into which his determination to see her in person has thrown him. Only in some enchanted form could he see her before his very eyes without abandoning the lovely image forged by his fancy.

In the long run, the enchantment perpetrated by Sancho will do his master more harm than good; but, as has already been suggested, for a while his madness will contrive to use it as a shield. One day the Duchess mentions how, on reading that Sancho found Dulcinea winnowing wheat, there lodged in her mind a scruple about the quality of Dulcinea's lineage. Only too well does Don Quixote know that he is pursued by enemy enchanters who, seeing they cannot hurt him in his person, avenge themselves on him by mistreating his lady. This is how he reacts to the Duchess's scruple: "So I believe that when my squire took my message to her, they converted her into a low-born wench occupied in the menial task of winnowing wheat." What proofs can he allege to support his belief? Why, "in proof of this truth, I wish to tell your Highnesses how coming recently through El Toboso, I was never able to find Dulcinea's palaces; and the next day Sancho saw her as her very self, which is the most beautiful in the world, while to me she seemed a rough and ugly peasant girl. . . . I have said all this so that no one will pay any attention to what Sancho said about Dulcinea's winnowing and sifting; because if they transformed her for me, it is not to be wondered at that they might change her for him. Dulcinea is noble and well-born, belonging to one of the principal families of El Toboso" (II. 32). Note how Dulcinea's plebian appearance leads on to the establishment of her noble lineage!

This is, give or take a little, the history of the stratagems

used by Don Quixote's madness to defend his chivalric illusions. How can one fail to take seriously a madness that
defends its illusions with such tenacity and cunning? [15] If
it defends itself heroically, may it not be because it senses
that the consequences of defeat will prove fatal?

Nearly forty years ago Salvador de Madariaga wrote a
fine book about *Don Quixote,* from which I wish now to
recall two sentences: "During the whole of his heroic life,
Don Quixote will carry in his soul this doubt, this inner
enemy, the most formidable he ever fought, the one that
finally conquered him and took away his joy in living"; and
the similar: "Maker of his own glory, Don Quixote har-
bored in his soul the enemy most to be feared: intimate
awareness that all was illusion." [16] Long after the publication
of Madariaga's book, Alberto Navarro González published
an essay specifically on Don Quixote's madness. In it he
alludes to Madariaga's work, but not to agree with his
point of view: "Furthermore, it does not seem to us correct
to suppose in Don Quixote an intimate doubt or belief that
all was illusion, an awareness of his own insanity. This he
acquires only on his deathbed, and we know that at that
moment he will cease to be Don Quixote to become again
Alonso Quijano . . . It is true that Don Quixote repeatedly
manifests doubts, but these never deal with the core of his
madness (reality of the chivalric world and of his own per-
sonality, lawfulness and urgency of his undertaking), and
much less with the madness that possesses him." [17] Toward

15. It is possible that some reader may wonder whether it makes
sense to take seriously certain reasonings of Don Quixote that are clearly
touched with irony—those, for example, that argue the choice between
imitating Roland or Amadis. We know that one of his reasons for not
imitating Roland was because to do so might seem to impute Angelica's
infidelity to Dulcinea. As he defends Dulcinea in his mind against such
a charge, he thinks that "she is as intact as the mother who bore her"
(I. 26). This and other similar ironies in Don Quixote's speech belong
to Cervantes. I find no evidence that Don Quixote is conscious of any
of them.

16. *Guía del lector del Quijote* (Madrid: Espasa-Calpe, 1926), p. 122.

17. "La locura quijotesca," *Anales Cervantinos,* 1 (1951), 277.

which of these two points of view does the evidence point? The answer may be found by sketching the history of the crumbling of Don Quixote's illusions, which is also the history of his progress toward sanity and death.

When Don Quixote sets out upon the roads of Spain to fulfill his knightly mission, he believes fully in it and in knight-errantry. He neither knows he is mad nor doubts the wisdom of his decision to revive in his own person the order of chivalry. He is disposed to explain his mission and defend the truth of knighthood to all who come his way. Besides, he possesses the spirit and imagination to transform the world, so that where others see only windmills, sheep, and prosaic travelers, he may find knightly adventures. But gradually, ever so gradually, all this begins to change.

Our hero's decline in energy and spirit is marked in Part II and wants little demonstrating. On this third sally Don Quixote creates less than half the adventures realized on the first two.[18] He no longer converts inns into castles.[19] Once —inconceivable conduct for him!—he flees from danger and becomes more reasonable.[20] He even pays with money for damages occasioned by his actions, as in the adventure of Master Peter's puppet show (II. 26) and that of the enchanted boat (II. 29).

But even before Don Quixote suffered any loss of dash and determination, he began to be troubled by certain doubts, although at first they did not attack the marrow of his madness. Perhaps his first serious doubt was whether or not the age is propitious for the revival of chivalry. After the depressing adventure of the fulling mills, master and man converse about a number of matters, including the salary

18. This may be somewhat explained—but only somewhat—by the fact that in Part II some of his adventures are contrived by Sansón Carrasco, the Duke, etc.

19. Three times in Part II he explicitly recognizes inns and taverns as such (II. 24, 59, 71).

20. In the presence of the threatening crossbows and harquebuses of the braying town (II. 27). Long before, he had expressed the abhorrence inspired in him by "the diabolical invention of firearms" (I. 38).

the latter is to receive if the time for favors never comes. Note what Don Quixote says: "If I have specified it [payment] for you in the closed will I left at home, it was on account of the way things might turn out; because I still don't know how chivalry will turn out in these calamitous times, and I wouldn't want my soul to suffer in the other world for such small matters" (I. 20). Then, at the inn, when he pronounces his famous speech on arms and letters, he again treats the same subject, and this time with more feeling. He has just called attention to artillery's frightful fury: "And so, considering this, I am inclined to say that it grieves my soul to have embarked upon the exercise of knight-errantry in an age as detestable as this in which we live" (I. 38). Here he carries his first statement to the point of questioning momentarily the wisdom of his own decision to become a knight. And then, toward the end of his last sally, in the presence of some carved images of saints which they encountered shortly after leaving the palace of the Duke and Duchess, Don Quixote comes finally to doubt the efficacy of his mission: "They conquered Heaven by force of arms, because Heaven suffereth violence, but up till now I know not what I conquer by force of my labors" (II. 58).

Before experiencing doubts of his own, Don Quixote has to face the doubts and scoffings of others. Cervantes does not say explicitly to what degree these alien doubts affect the spirit of his hero. At first they do not seem to affect him at all, and he is disposed to explain them away to doubters willing to listen, but little by little he learns caution and reserve. In speaking with Dorotea, after hearing Sancho affirm that she is only a private damsel and the slain giant but a punctured wineskin, he says in reference to the latter: "because it was only a few hours ago that I encountered him, and . . . I will be silent lest they say I lie; but time, the discoverer of all things, will speak out when we least expect it" (I. 37). On noticing that the Canon of Toledo and his retinue are curious about his encagement, Don Quixote says, "Gentlemen, are your Graces perchance versed and skilled in matters of knighthood? Because, if you are, I will communicate my misfortunes to you; and if not, there is no point in my troubling to tell them" (I. 47). Realizing in time that his figure arouses wonder in all who encounter him, and feeling some inner need to justify it, he anticipates the curiosity of Don Diego de Miranda and explains his profession to him. When the latter refers to fictitious knights, Don Quixote replies, "There is much to be said about whether or not the histories of knights-errant are fictitious." Don Diego rejoins, "But, does anyone doubt such histories are false?" " 'I doubt it,' answered Don Quixote, 'and let the matter rest here' " (II. 16). Finally, in response to doubt expressed by Don Diego's son, Don Quixote sums up his experiences thus: "Many times have I said what I now repeat . . . that most of the people in the world are of the opinion that there have never been knights-errant in it; and since it seems to me that, unless Heaven miraculously gives them to understand that there have been and are, any effort I may make will be in vain, as experience has often shown me; I do not wish to take the time now to extract your Grace from the error you share with the many" (II. 18).

As we have already noted, Don Quixote did not know he was mad when he launched his chivalric career; when on his deathbed he recovers his sanity, he recognizes explicitly his past madness. Besides what we have said about the doubts and lessons experience has taught him, what other milestones mark the slow road leading from Don Quixote to Alonso Quijano?

When Sancho, before embarking on his mission to Dulcinea, explains with genuine irritation what he intends to do if she refuses to give him a proper answer, Don Quixote remarks: "you are no saner than I am" (I. 25). In thus obliquely confessing his own lack of sanity, it may be that he is thinking only of the deliberately chosen madness of his intended penance in Sierra Morena. There is no way of being certain. What is certain is his eventual realization that he may seem mad to others. Two times some uneasy stirrings in the depths of his consciousness move him to explain himself to Don Diego de Miranda. The second time he introduces his explanation with these words: "Who doubts, Don Diego de Miranda, that your Grace takes me for an absurd and demented man? And it would be no wonder if you did, since my deeds can bear witness to nothing less. Still and all, I want your Grace to notice that I am not so mad or foolish as I must have seemed to you" (II. 17). This quasi confession of madness is a marker on the path to recovered sanity. Another may be found in the words he pronounced before the images of the three saints: "but if my Dulcinea del Toboso should escape from those labors she suffers, my luck being improved and my senses restored, it might be that I would set my steps on a better road than the one I am following" (II. 58).[21]

It seems that at this juncture in his inner life our knight hopes for three things: better luck, restored senses, and a new direction. It may be well to recall here some of the circumstances of Don Quixote's life at the time he speaks the revealing words just quoted. The Knight of the White Moon has not yet defeated him. Apparently nothing serious has just occurred. What then prompts such profound intuition at just this time? We have already insinuated that a

---

21. Unamuno cites this entire passage and devotes several pages of commentary to it. His first sentence indicates the tenor of his interpretation: "Profound passage! Here the temporal madness of the Knight Don Quixote dissolves in the eternal goodness of the gentleman Alonso the Good's sanity, and in the whole sad epic of his life there is perhaps no passage that so deeply grieves his heart" (*Vida de Don Quijote y Sancho*, p. 324).

decisive role in Don Quixote's progressive disillusionment was played by the fictitious life certain people contrive to make him live in Part II. He speaks the words we have been considering just after leaving the palace of the Duke and Duchess, where he has unwittingly led, for their amusement, a counterfeit existence. The spiritual relief experienced on abandoning that existence can be sensed in his heart-felt tribute to liberty.[22]

There are still other signs that something portentous is stirring in the depths of Don Quixote's spirit: a growing and unaccustomed ill humor and many imaginings and sad thoughts. From the day he leaves Don Diego's house until the conclusion of everything connected with Camacho's wedding, he manifests a constant irritation with Sancho, and this despite his recent triumphs over the Knight of the Mirrors and over the lions. Here, for example, are Don Quixote's ill-natured words addressed to Sancho: "Where will you end, Sancho, damn you? . . . When you start stringing proverbs and tales together, nobody can wait for you but Judas himself—may he carry you off! Tell me, animal, what do you know about spikes or wheels or anything else?" (II. 19). Or: "For God's sake, Sancho, have done with your harangue" (II. 20). Or: "Would to God, Sancho . . . that I may see you mute before I die" (II. 20). Given other similar examples, are the overabundant proverbs and the garrulity of Sancho really sufficient cause for so much bad humor? Probably not. Don Quixote behaves like a man preoccupied and melancholy, and it seems possible to locate the exact fountain from which his melancholy preoccupations issue.

22. The following is a fragment of this tribute: "I say this, Sancho, because you have seen the abundance with which we have been regaled in this castle we have had to leave; well, in the midst of those well-seasoned banquets and snow-cooled drinks, it seemed to me that I was caught in the clutches of hunger, because I did not enjoy them with the freedom that I would if they were mine; since obligations to return benefits and favors received are bonds that fetter a free spirit" (II. 58).

When Sancho departed for El Toboso to seek Dulcinea's palaces, "Don Quixote remained mounted, resting on his stirrups and leaning on his lance, full of sad and confused imaginings, where we will leave him while we accompany Sancho" (II. 10). How are these sad and confused imaginings to be accounted for? At the very least, they may seem premature, since Don Quixote cannot know that Sancho is going to enchant Dulcinea. Does he already suspect beneath the surface of his consciousness that his determination to see in person the lady of his dreams has trapped him in a labyrinth from which no escape is possible? Be this as it may, here starts a train of imaginings and sad thoughts which will carry him even to his deathbed. On seeing Dulcinea's ill-fated transmutation, he exclaims, "I was born to be the exemplar of unfortunate men" (II. 10). Shortly after, he repeats himself: "Now I say again, and shall say a thousand times, that I am the most unfortunate of men" (II. 10). Then the narrator stresses the knight's preoccupation: "Deep in sorrowful thought, Don Quixote went his way, considering the evil trick the enchanters had played on him in changing his lady Dulcinea into the uncouth figure of a peasant girl, and he couldn't imagine what remedy would serve to restore her to her pristine self; and these thoughts so distracted him that he gave Rocinante his head without knowing it" (II. 11).

Henceforth the worry of this misfortune will never leave him, and to it will be added many others large and small. In the palace of the Duke and Duchess there were the run in his stockings and Altisidora's amorous harassment of his peace of mind: "We left the great Don Quixote wrapt in the thoughts that the music of the enamored damsel Altisidora had aroused in him. He went to bed with them, and as though they were fleas, they did not allow him to sleep or rest a stitch, and to them were added those of his damaged stockings" (II. 46). And the cat-scratching he suffered: "Excessively cross and melancholy was the sorely-wounded Don Quixote, his face bandaged and marked, not by the hand of God but by the claws of a cat . . . Six days he remained without appearing in public; on one of those nights, being awake and watchful, thinking about his misfortunes and Altisidora's persecution . . ." (II. 48). Later, on the road, he is trampled, kicked, and bruised by a herd of fighting bulls. Sancho recovers promptly from this mishap and wants to eat. Enveloped in mournful imaginings, Don Quixote does not eat but invites Sancho to do so, saying, "Eat, friend Sancho . . . sustain life, which matters more to you than to me, and let me die at the hands of my thoughts and by the force of my misfortunes" (II. 59). On the road to Barcelona master and man enter a wood to pass the night, but Don Quixote, "whose imaginings kept him awake more than his hunger, could not sleep a wink; rather, he came and went with his thoughts through a thousand places." His thoughts turned, above all, to the disenchantment of Dulcinea, and "he grew desperate over the laxity and lack of charity of his squire Sancho." In the morning Roque Guinart finds him "pensive, with the most doleful and melancholy countenance that sadness itself might form" (II. 60). And then the crowning misfortune: his decisive defeat at the hands of the Knight of the White Moon. This is how Cervantes describes his condition: "Six days Don Quixote remained in bed, sick, sad, thoughtful, and in a bad way, pondering in his imagination the unhappy event of his defeat" (II. 65).

Disarmed at last, Don Quixote rides slowly homeward. As he passes the site of his defeat, he exclaims, "Here fell Troy! Here my misfortune, not my cowardice, carried off the glory of my achievements; here Fortune worked her shifts and changes on me; here were my great deeds obscured; here did my happiness fall, never to rise again" (II. 61). He has lost now for good the shield of his chivalric illusions. When they ask for his opinion—he who had been so fond of offering opinions—he wants Sancho to answer and he says, "I am not fit to give crumbs to a cat, my mind is so shaken and upset" (II. 61). And now his mournful thoughts redouble their attack: "If many thoughts fatigued Don Quixote before he was overcome, many more fatigued him after his fall. He was waiting in the shade of a tree, as has been said, and there, like flies around honey, his thoughts swarmed about him and stung him: some pointed at Dulcinea's disenchantment, others at the life he would lead in his enforced retirement" (II. 67).

On passing through the meadow where they came upon "the elegant shepherdesses and gallant shepherds who wished to revive and imitate pastoral Arcadia" (II. 67), it occurs to Don Quixote, in his madness, to substitute a pastoral illusion for the chivalric illusion now thwarted. His mind toys with this notion for a while, but it seems to be too late for a new and saving illusion to possess him. His life's trajectory is declining with an impetus now irreversible. That same night he and his squire are trampled by a herd of filthy swine. This time Don Quixote does not try to pursue them as he did the fighting bulls on an earlier occasion. Afterward, while Sancho sleeps, he unburdens his grief by singing a madrigal, whose verses are accompanied by tears, as though of one "whose heart was pierced with the sorrow of defeat and the absence of Dulcinea" (II. 68). The following day some of the Duke's servants seize him and Sancho and take them to the castle, where they are subjected to one more round of counterfeit incidents like those of their previous visit there and to the house of Don Antonio Moreno in Barcelona.

Finally, they reach the outskirts of their town, where Don Quixote sees evil omens, which he interprets to mean that he is never to see Dulcinea again. Sancho tries to discredit the omens, but his master does not respond to his efforts. On reaching home, Don Quixote tells the Priest and the Barber of his defeat and of his pastoral projects, and then goes to bed to rise no more. And "his end came when he least expected it; because whether it was the melancholy caused by seeing himself conquered or simply the disposition of Heaven, which ordered it so, a fever seized him and kept him in bed for six days" (II. 74). His squire and his other friends visited him repeatedly and tried to lift his spirits by talking to him of the pastoral exercises they had projected, "but not on that account did he abandon his sorrow" (II. 74), until at last, after a long sleep, he woke up with his mind clear and free. And in three days he died, having made his will and received all the sacraments.

In the light of all these passages, what shall we say of the recovered sanity and death of Don Quixote? First, we must not forget that his madness and his knightly illusions are so inextricably interwoven that for him to recover his senses would mean to lose his illusions; also, that he tried to substitute pastoral illusions for chivalric ones but without success.

As we said earlier, one of the illusions dearest to our knight's heart was that of serving a great lady. This illusion ran no serious risk until he attempted to see her in person, at which point she remained enchanted forever. Now it would be impossible to disenchant her even if Sancho should apply to his own skin rather than to the bark of trees the 3,300 lashes prescribed by Merlin. In his subconscious mind Don Quixote must have sensed this, because he reached his village without hope of seeing her again.

Another part of Don Quixote's chivalric ideal was to win good fame. When he conveyed to the Duke and Duchess his worry over Dulcinea's enchantment, he foretold the destruction of his fame: "Persecuted have I been by enchanters, enchanters persecute me, and enchanters will persecute me until they cast me and my high knightly deeds into oblivion's deep abyss" (II. 32). And he considers this destruction accomplished after his defeat on the strand at Barcelona. Note the already cited passage in which he said that his misfortune had obscured his great deeds and swept away the glory of his achievements.

One of the conditions of the combat between Don Quixote and the Knight of the White Moon was that the defeated combatant would abandon the exercise of knight-errantry for a period of one year or more.[23] With his defeat in this battle, then, Don Quixote is barred from exercising the third part of his ideal, which was to succor the needy and the wronged. And so the doors to the three essential parts of his ideal are locked.

Don Quixote resists very well casual mishaps and even frontal attacks. He may be discouraged briefly or annoyed for a while, but always he is able to recover his equanimity and hold to his chivalric course. What he cannot successfully cope with is the insidious undermining of his illusions, and that is how they are destroyed. As though in a Trojan horse, his friends and acquaintances penetrate the walls of his illusions, where no defense is possible. A knight without a lady is like a building without a foundation. Don Quixote loses his lady by a process—enchantment—in harmony with his illusions but ultimately fatal to his status as a true knight. And Sansón Carrasco contrives to beat him in a battle whose agreed-upon terms foreclose his knightly future. The certainty of this foreclosure is suggested by the confident words spoken by Carrasco to Don Antonio Moreno after the battle: "And since he is so punctual in observing the orders of chivalry, without any doubt he will observe the order I have given him" (II. 65). Thus, by virtue of Don Quixote's

23. In reality, the period could be extended indefinitely. Here are the final words of the Knight of the White Moon on the subject: "I'll be satisfied if the great Don Quixote retires to his village for a year, or until such time as I command, as we agreed before entering this battle" (II. 64).

knightly principles, it is possible to slam the door of knight-hood in his face. He does not abandon his illusions: he is thrown out of them, and not without injury to his spirit.

Our knight returns home bruised in body and in spirit. His body has suffered physical hardships such as are not often borne by a man of his age, and his spirit has endured the uncomfortable feignings of frivolous people and the shock of final defeat. His chivalric ideal gave him both a reason for living and a program of action, and now it is gone. How, then, can one doubt the plausibility of his death?

At the beginning of this chapter we asked whether it is possible to present madness as authentic human experience and at the same time make it serve the ends of parody. We then tried to demonstrate that Cervantes has succeeded in presenting Don Quixote's madness as authentic human experience, but nothing we have said is meant to suggest that his madness is not also an instrument of parody. If there is, as some critics seem to believe, any incompatibility between the two functions, it does not apply to Cervantes. In this, as in so many other things, he is one of those rare artists who, as the Spanish saying goes, are able to ring the church bells and walk in the procession too.

EPILOGUE

*D*ON QUIXOTE SHAPES his new life in a world where literature is a constant presence. Literature, being merely a representation of life, stands in contrast to Don Quixote's life, which thus seems entirely real. But literature fulfills other functions as well: it is a fountain of illusions and projects, without which the life we call human would be inconceivable, since to be human is to be ever prone to follow the light of one's dreams and illusions. Don Quixote discovered his illusions in the literature of chivalry, and by their light he was able to find adventures otherwise impossible. For the most part, the adventures spring from the clash of illusions and reality. As reality often resists being molded by illusion, it may be a source of disillusion. But Don Quixote, like all who act in the name of the Good, expected to have to contend with powerful, if sometimes invisible, agents of Evil; and this expectation helped him to understand and endure the trials of recurrent defeat.

In Don Quixote's world he is not the only one to follow the light of his illusions, nor is he the only one whose dealings with reality sometimes prove frustrating. And the truth is that reality is something of a siren who promises more than she fulfills. It is not uncommon for reality to offer appearances that seem to authorize interpretations altogether extraordinary; furthermore, it is always possible to find in reality more uses than have been catalogued. In short, a man may always discover along the edges of his life some margin of undefined reality; and this is all the leeway he needs to animate the inventions of his fantasy.

In a certain sense, then, it may be said that Don Quixote lives his madness in a world tending to justify it. The illusions that come so naturally to man, and the puzzling appearances that reality may assume, allow it to flourish as a plant entirely human. In spite of his striking originality, our knight shows nothing of the monster—neither Quevedo nor Goya, but Cervantes.

In Don Quixote's world there are pranks and mortifications, hardships and defeats, disillusion and death. Is the flickering light that men follow, then, merely a will-o'-the-wisp? Are illusions forged only to be shattered against the unyielding world? For Cervantes the answer would seem to be No. He created a spacious world charged with potentiality—a realm where wanton wenches could become ladies-in-waiting, and barbers' basins, royal helmets; above all, an open world whose rare freedom serves not the triumph of matter but the revelation of spirit.

INDEX

Abindarráez, 9n
Agramante, 68
Alemán, Mateo, 9n
Alquife, 51
Altisidora, 49, 81, 90, 122, 123
Amadís of Gaul, 50, 106, 107, 116n
Ana Félix, 79
Andrés, 17, 18, 19, 20, 21, 28, 58, 101
Angelica, 107
Anselmo, 83, 85, 93, 94, 96
Arcadia, 2, 45, 124
Arcalaus, 50
Avellaneda, 14, 50n
Azorín, 99
Azpeitia, Don Sancho. See Basque

Bachelor. See Carrasco, Sansón
Barber, 10, 25, 32, 43, 62, 88, 93, 125
Barcelona, 10, 37, 48, 78, 123, 124
Basilio, 45, 52, 97
Basque, 18, 20, 21, 22, 25, 29, 36, 54, 80
Bates, Margaret J., 63
Benedictine friars, 36, 38, 54, 55
Benedictine giants. See Benedictine friars
Biscayan. See Basque
Briareuses, 55
Britton, Karl, 34n

Cabrera, Fray Alonso de, 97
Camacho the Rich, 45, 77
Camila, 85, 90, 91, 94, 95
Candaya, 80
Canon of Toledo: critical of Don Quixote's reading, 7-8; on chivalric literature, 9; Spanish theater, 9, 32, 43, 103, 104, 110, 119
Captive Captain, 10, 23n, 66, 76, 95
Cardenio, 12, 67, 76, 85, 89, 91, 92, 95, 96n
Carrasco, Sansón, 11, 12, 13, 25, 39, 40, 46, 52, 55, 62, 65, 90, 92, 96, 117n, 126
Castro, Américo, 2, 18, 19, 53, 57n, 94, 97n, 99, 112n
Catholic faith, 33
Cecial, Tomé, 46, 65, 92
Cervantes: stepfather of Don Quixote, 3; and chance, 23n; and impressionistic language, 57-67 passim, 75-79 passim; and language of conjecture, 69-75 passim, 80-81; and language of approximation, 78-80
Christian religion, 102, 105
Cide Hamete Benengeli, 4-7, 93, 97
Clara, Doña, 78
Clavileño, 23, 24, 25, 26, 47, 65, 111
Clorinia, 9n

Daraja, 9n
Desengaño de celos, 10n
Diana, La, 9n
Dolorida, La. See Trifaldi, Countess
Don Quixote: well-known in La Mancha, 3; surnames, 3-4, 80, 116; mad from reading books of chivalry, 7-8; his library, 10; literary recognition as fame, 11; air of autonomous reality, 12-14; adventures, 17-35; successes and failures in Part I, 19-20, in Part II, 26-27; first sally, 28; and test of palpability, 34n; and enchantment, 36-40; called Knight of the Sad Countenance, 73, 93; how he went mad, 99-100; concept of chivalry, 101-105; God-given mission, 103; defends illusions, 104-116 passim; progress toward sanity and death, 117-127
Don Quixote: function of literature

Index

in, 1–16 *passim;* moral order in, 18–27 *passim;* operation of chance in, 22; characters not instruments in, 25; enchantment in, 36–52; reality in, 54–83; illusions in, 84–97; as parody of romances of chivalry, 98, 127; as study of madness, 98–127 *passim*

Dorido, 9n

Dorotea, 23n, 39, 40, 57, 75, 82, 86, 92, 94, 95, 118

Duchess, 12, 13, 23n, 25, 26, 48, 49, 52, 67, 81, 83, 86, 89, 97, 105, 110n, 118, 121, 122, 125

Duke, 23n, 25, 26, 52, 81, 86, 94, 97, 105, 110n, 117n, 118, 121, 122, 124, 125

Dulcinea del Toboso, 13, 14, 20, 39, 40, 47, 48, 57, 58, 64, 65, 78, 82, 88, 92, 106, 107, 110, 111, 113, 114, 115, 116, 119, 120, 122, 123, 124, 125; importance to Don Quixote, 101

Durandarte, 111

Ebro River, 38

Erasmus, 100

Felicia, 9n

Felixmartes of Hyrcania, 8

Fernando, 23n, 68, 92

Fichter, William, 57n

Freston, 36, 38, 51, 60, 111

Garcilaso de la Vega, 110

Gillet, Joseph E., 3n

Ginés de Pasamonte, 2, 32

God, 102

Golden Age, discourse on, 90

Gombrich, E. H., 35n

Goya, 129

Granada, 99

Gregorio, Don, 56, 79

Green, Otis H., 98n

Grisóstomo, 2, 75, 78, 91

Guinart, Roque, 12, 78, 90, 96, 123

Guzmán de Alfarache, 9n

Helen (of Troy), 113

Holy Brotherhood, the, 32, 41, 43, 64, 68

Housekeeper, 10

Huarte de San Juan, 98

Jerónima, Claudia, 78, 91

Jesus, 105n

Judas, 121

Knight-Errant, story of the, 109

Knight of the Green Coat. *See* Miranda, Don Diego de

Knight of the Lake, story of the, 110

Knight of the Mirrors (Sansón Carrasco), 62, 64–65, 121

Knight of the Sad Countenance. *See* Don Quixote

Knight of the White Moon (Sansón Carrasco), 23, 24, 25, 26, 49, 65–66, 78, 120, 123, 126

Knight of the Wood (Sansón Carrasco), 23, 24, 26, 39, 40, 46, 87

Lazarillo de Tormes, 2

Leandra, 45, 52, 91

Leonela, 90

Lindner, Robert, 98n

Lirgandeo, 51

Lorenzo, Aldonza, 57, 113

Lorenzo, Don, 96

Lothario, 77, 85, 87, 90, 91, 94, 95, 96

Lucretia, 114

Luis, Don, 67, 86, 97

Luscinda, 66, 76, 85, 91, 96, 97

Madariaga, Salvador de, 116

Malambruno, 51

Mambrino's helmet, 11, 18, 20, 31, 39, 40, 54, 60, 109

Man Too Curious for His Own Good, The, 9, 10, 42, 83, 87

Mancha, La, 2–3, 99, 113

Manchegan Knight. *See* Don Quixote

Mann, Thomas, 98

Maritornes, 36, 41, 66

Mathew, 105n

Index

Merlin, 51
Micomicón, 111
Micomicona, Princess, 20, 39, 40, 43, 89
Miranda, Don Diego de, 62, 77, 78, 80n, 105n, 119, 120, 121
Montesinos, Cave of, 23, 24, 26, 33n, 44n, 48, 64, 77, 110n, 111
Montesinos (knight), 111
Moor, the enchanted, 41, 46, 54
Moors, land of the, 76, 99
Moreno, Don Antonio, 25, 87, 124, 126

Navarro González, Alberto, 116
Niece, Don Quixote, 10
Ninfas y pastores de Henares, 10n

Ozmín, 9n

Palomeque, Juan, 8, 36
Pandafilando, 32, 42
Panza. See Sancho Panza
Parker, A. A., 54n
"Parliament of Death, The," 23, 24, 26, 33n, 34, 61
Pensamiento de Cervantes, El, 53
Peter, Master (Ginés de Pasamonte), 23, 40, 76, 86, 117
Priest, 10, 25, 32, 43, 49, 57, 86, 88, 93, 112, 125; on chivalric literature, 9; on Spanish theater, 9

Quejana. See Don Quixote
Quesada. See Don Quixote
Quevedo, 129
Quijada. See Don Quixote
Quijana. See Don Quixote
Quijano, Alonso. See Don Quixote
Quiteria, 45, 81
Quixote. See Don Quixote

Rocinante, 22, 25, 38, 57, 75
Rodríguez, Doña, 5, 26, 39, 40, 48, 67, 77

Roland, 106, 107, 116n

Saint Benedict, order of, 29
Saint George, 76
Sancho Panza: well-known in La Mancha, 3; air of autonomous reality, 12–14; and enchantment, 41–46; called Sancho Zancas, 80, 81
Segovia, 55
Sierra Morena, 32, 37, 47, 59, 85, 88, 95, 106, 120
Silva, Feliciano de, 57
Sobrino, King, 68
Spitzer, Leo, 13

Tagus River, 110
Tarfe, Don Alvaro, 48
Teresa Panza, 49, 86, 89
Tirante el Blanco, 8
Toboso, El, 21, 37, 47, 102, 113, 115, 122
Tosilos, 23, 24, 26, 39, 48, 93
Toledo, 4, 17, 18, 21, 24, 28
Trebizond, 8
Trifaldi, Countess, 5, 39, 40, 46, 65, 82, 86, 110n
Trojan horse, 126
Troy, 123

Uchalí, 90
Unamuno, Miguel de, 14n, 120n
Urganda the Unknown, 50

Vilanova, Antonio, 100
Virgin Mary, 32
Vivaldo, 66, 75, 90, 102, 113

Wardropper, Bruce W., 4n
Willis, R. S., Jr., 6–7

Yanguesans, 46, 54

Zancas, Sancho. See Sancho Panza
Zoraida, 67